A Garden of Qualities

Living a Quality Life

Joanna Infeld

Printed in the United States of America

Kora Press ® is a federally registered trademark.

ISBN (10) 0-9815509-8-3
ISBN (13) 978-0-9815509-8-5

Cover photo by author:
Japanese Garden and Stud Farm,
Co. Kildare, Ireland
Garden vignettes by Ari Hoffman

K O R A
P R E S S

Published by Kora Press ®
www.KoraPress.com

Contents:

A Garden of Qualities

INTRODUCTION

*T*his book is about qualities—the traits of character a person develops throughout their life by what they do, how they think and the emotions they allow themselves to have or become subject to. Every person can be described by their qualities, or, to use two more old-fashioned words, by their virtues and their vices. Both these character attributes define a person, but this book is only concerned with virtues or with those qualities that belong at the high end of the energy worlds spectrum.

Qualities are energetic properties. They exist in the world's energetic field and get added to every day as we humans continue to think, be and do. There is a whole range of levels of energy that a person can connect to at any given moment. Throughout our day our responses to our environment and our interactions with others probably range from higher to lower and back again, depending on our strength of character, determination, upbringing and any number of other influences that have made us the person we are today.

A Tibetan nun or lama who lives in seclusion and meditates daily is perhaps less subject to the vicissitudes of the energies of the many qualities that exist in the world. But in a modern city there are thousands of negative energies floating around that are ready to claim a person when their guard is down and they can become subject to an unexpected altercation or chance encounter. Although more rare, there are also positive qualities available within the energy field of the planet we live on—qualities like patience, care, compassion and love. These are the qualities this book is concerned with. The author believes that by contemplating these qualities and understanding better their energetic blueprint and hallmarks, it will be easier for a person to connect to them and have them live within one's energetic field. For every time we act in, say, a courageous way, a little bit of courage stays in our aura and it is that much easier for us to connect to courage the next time a need for courage might arise.

This book is designed for you to pick up and dip into at your leisure. Perhaps it can help you develop the qualities you desire or enhance the qualities you have already invited into your life by your thoughts, actions and behaviors.

Part One

Living a Quality Life

CHAPTER ONE

The Quality of Life

A quality life is an elusive description of what one might perceive as a superior life. But how does one get there? How can one become a quality person or a person of quality? One way to achieve this is to deliberately aim one's efforts at collecting qualities. It is a bit like planting flowers in the garden—qualities need to be nurtured and grown before they can take root and develop into fully established energies that will enhance a person's radiation and influence all who come into contact with them.

Qualities are also known as virtues. Virtuosity is a word derived from the same root as the word virtue. To develop virtuosity, like learning to play an instrument well, one needs to practice for many hours with persistence and dedication. In his book *The Outliers*, Malcolm Gladwell suggests that it takes 10,000 hours before one can become proficient at anything. Therefore in one lifetime one only has enough time to become an expert at one or two skills or subjects.

But as far as qualities are concerned, it need not take that long to have the essence of, say, peace or gratitude reside within one's energetic field. To build a quality one can start with a quality or qualities one had acquired as a child—having learned to become host to it or them simply by being brought up in a specific home where that quality was valued and practiced. So someone who was brought up to have a respect for animals, for example, will carry that respect into their adult years and will not need to work for it or to deliberately practice it for it to be there every time they see a dog, a cat, a deer or a bird. It will come naturally to them and without effort. These natural qualities that each person possesses can then form the foundation upon which other qualities can be added. There are qualities that belong together and it is relatively easy to have peace, for example, if one has already adopted serenity as one's energetic companion. Or courage will come easily if one has a history of being brave. Or warmth will be a natural attribute of someone who is loving and kind.

One might think that contemplating the meaning of, for example, wisdom will not cause a person to necessarily be wise. But in researching the word—the meaning of the word as well as the mechanics of how the quality comes to be part of a person's energetic makeup—creates a frequency that is akin to the quality itself and promotes an openness for it to attach itself to the person's energy field.

If I am interested in, say, generosity and I spend time thinking about it and wondering about it, I will put myself on its frequency. Just like a person who is thinking of buying a Volkswagen car will start seeing Volkswagens everywhere they go, so will a person researching generosity begin to notice it in the behavior of people they know, or in little acts of kindness they witness as they go about their day. From there it is only another step to becoming generous oneself. Being sensitive to its manifestation and by studying the mechanics of how it works, one can easily take on the attitude that lies behind the generous acts one witnesses. We see what we want to see and what we have been educated to see, and we copy behaviors we find attractive. If I am attracted to generosity in others, I will want to become generous myself. In order to adopt the quality of generosity, all I need to do is become generous and perform generous act. Other people will then witness my actions and confirm them, thus adding to the power of my adopted quality.

Qualities are a gift from the gods. They are like the ambrosia which was stolen by Ganymede and added to the planet's water supply, to be consumed by humans. They bring with them joy, rejuvenation and healing. They allow a person to escape worry, depression and the drudgery of daily life.

Qualities are free and freely available. All the more so since not everyone values them or strives to welcome them into their life. They are all around us and await only our effort and dedication to come to assist and to join us in our endeavors.

Mother Teresa was the embodiment of charity and compassion, but those qualities defied some people's expectations about them. She was one tough lady, able to fight for what she perceived to be necessary to keep these qualities alive. Having decided to promote these qualities and embody them, it became her sacred duty to maintain that connection and fulfill her calling. We, too, can choose the qualities we wish to facilitate into the world and promote, becoming their midwives and guardians. However, once we adopt a quality, we might be surprised at the prices we will need to pay to maintain it and to provide the energetic environment it needs to thrive. We might also find that the energy accompanying a specific quality, once invited into our life and part of our energy field, can cause behaviors that surprise us.

A quality life is a life which brings with it self-awareness and self-value. It is a life of adventure and self-discovery. It is a life whose energy field is in constant flux as one adopts new qualities into one's energy field and creates circumstances within which they can flourish and grow.

CHAPTER TWO

Qualites Are Energies

*T*his book is an exploration of qualities from the standpoint of their energetic content. Qualities are manifestations of energy—they existed before humans walked and lived on this Earth and continue to be an integral part of universal life as it appears in space as well as on all planets, suns, moons, stars and galaxies. For are the planets not constant in their revolutionary journeys around the sun and does the Earth not display loyalty and courage in her consistent support of all life that has been entrusted to her? Love exists, as does compassion, constancy, patience and forgiveness, independent of us humans, but added to and processed by human endeavors every single moment of every single day. Humans are late comers to this cosmic table of plenty; we (or some of us) are still learning to connect to and process qualities in order to have a quality life.

To dwell on qualities is to put yourself on their frequency. A quality is an energy—it recognizes its frequency. When you act in a way that is defined by a specific quality, that quality will come to reside in your energy field in response. When a person connects to a quality, they are also connecting to the energy that accompanies that quality. That energy superimposes upon the energy that they were processing before. It is a simple situation within which one energy replaces another because lower and higher energies cannot live in the same place together at the same time. The same principle applies in an exorcism—if successful, a higher energy replaces the lower. In fact, every time a person connects to a higher energy and replaces a lower energy connection with a higher, they are performing a self-exorcism.

Qualities inhabit the higher energy worlds; they are gateways into higher energy realms. When affected by a lower energy connection it is sometimes difficult to find one's way out of that energetic fog that can surround one, obscuring one's view of reality. Being surrounded by lower energies can cause depression, worry or bring about any number of ailments or despondent moods. Once affected by lower energies, it can be hard to change one's state. People hire psychologists and therapists so they can help them adjust their point of view and hopefully climb out of depression or learn to manage their mood swings.

Qualities are a sure way to find a way out of lower energy states without the use of drugs or medications. Contemplate peace, for example, and it will be difficult to continue in an upset or angry state. Or contemplate forgiveness, and it will guide you away from blame. Each quality is an antidote to a number of lower-level energies. Qualities are natural companions to a life of quality; qualities and quality belong together. To have a life of quality, or a quality life, is to aim at quality in any situation and to bring specific qualities into one's energy field.

If a person acts courageously, for example, the energy of courage cannot not respond and attend them. So the next time they need a little bit of courage, it will come into their magnetic sphere that much more easily and quickly.

"Take courage," people say and it is indeed also possible to take hope or love or compassion or humility. How can that be? Because a quality exists as an electrical imprint or force field in the world. Courageous people have left an energetic trace and it is there to be tapped into, to be adopted. The longer human history unfolds, the more courageous acts continue to be performed and the more energy associated with courage there is to be connected to and emulated.

The author once accompanied a young girl who felt sick—maybe she had eaten something that did not agree with her. I had no idea what to do, but I thought of my friend who was a nurse and a very compassionate woman. As soon as I thought about her, I found within myself the patience and care to help the girl clean up, give her some soothing words, help her relax; and soon she felt much better. I believe it was not me doing this, but I had "borrowed" the intelligence accompanying the quality of compassion from my nurse friend.

What do you radiate or emanate? What you think about and do and have emotions about determines your radiation. If your radiation were visible, what would it look like? What color would it be? We often look best in colors that complement not only our skin tone, but also our energy radiation. What colors do you wear? What colors are missing from your wardrobe? What color is your favorite dress, blouse, shirt, top, coat etc.?

Our radiation has a frequency that draws to itself similar frequencies. We are most like people we like. Look at your closest friends—what are they like? What are their greatest strengths? Very likely you have some of the strengths that you admire in others. It takes a caring person, for example, to see and appreciate care in another.

Think of your work, your club, or any group you meet with on a regular basis. Who are the people who are drawn to you? What are they like? Do you like them or just tolerate them? What do they radiate? What qualities do they exhibit in their behavior? What is their conversation like? How do you feel after you meet them and exchange words with them? Start thinking of people as radiators of qualities. Their qualities define them so much better than their physical appearance. Appearances will change and physical beauty fades with age but qualities will most probably grow stronger as people grow older.

Everything radiates. In fact, matter is mostly empty space with electrical impulses between the vast expanses of nothingness. It is the radiation that determines the matter, not the other way around. "You become what you think about" has been a known adage for centuries. It will determine who you are, both in the material world as well as in the realms of energy, thought and action.

We can decide what we radiate, rather than being subject to or a mouthpiece for any stray essence that happens to be floating by. Energies can change with the weather and cause our moods to change with the season. Anger, for example, caused by a bad harvest in one country can relocate to a neighboring land and people there will feel malcontent without knowing the reasons why.

A person radiates the energies they are connected to. They also radiate their attachments to material possessions, to people, to places and to ideas. Their energy field contains their character formation which includes qualities, as well as their emotions, thinking, sexuality, creativity, instincts, habits and actions.

We are all a whole conglomerate of swirling masses of energy, forever changing, depending on our moods, feelings, hopes, desires and thought processes. Sometimes it is difficult to separate out what causes what and which energies are predominant at any given time. When someone meets us and shakes our hand or has a conversation with us, they are connecting to our energies and our history, as it lives in our energy field or aura.

To take charge of one's life is to decide what one will have and what one will not have within one's energy formations. Sometimes this means waiting until something crops up, like a negative emotion, before knowing that it is there and needs to be dealt with. Take anger, for example. A person might think they have no anger, but then one day it shows up in response to a situation or an encounter. That is when one can decide to deal with it. Once anger has become active within one's energy field, that is not the time to make important decisions about who, what and how one wants to be. This is the time to cool down and return to balance. Then, having experienced anger and the damaging effects it has on one's energetic state, one can decide to do something about it. The best way to deal with any negative emotion is to reason why one would want not to have it. Then to find ways—in the cool of the day—to deal with it when it does crop up. Counting to ten before responding is a classic example of how to deal with anger or any other explosive emotion that can take one by surprise. Another is to excuse oneself and go into a private space to "vent"—say a bathroom, where one can flush the negative energy down the toilet. A third way to deal with negative emotions is to deliberately attempt to connect to their opposite. So, for example, replacing anger with tolerance or anxiety with serenity could be a worthwhile pursuit.

We can decide what we want to radiate within our energy field. Say we decide to radiate warmth. The best way to put into practice one's deliberate radiation of a quality is to find actions and language that reflect that quality. So with warmth, for example, one would try to find terms of endearment, encouragement, while deliberately projecting warmth. Words and actions are like little packages of energy—we can decide what kind of energy we wish to send out into the world. It is like writing a letter and then adding stardust into the envelope. So, with warmth, for example, when talking with people, one could also project a warm color, like yellow or orange, with the words. One could use warming words and phrases, like words of appreciation and value for another person.

If, for example, one wishes to adopt the quality of compassion, it is not enough to be compassionate; one must also be seen to be compassionate in order for that quality to become augmented in one's energy field and in the energy fields of other people. Your compassionate actions and thoughts need to be witnessed not only by people, but by essences, the unseen worlds, flora, fauna, the planet, the universe—they are all witnesses to our lives and deeds and they all have their own intelligence. Our behavior is held by others within their memory and our history radiates back to us from those who have seen us and remember who we are.

So what does this mean for a person who wishes to connect to the energy of compassion? They need to not just feel compassion, which is compassion coming in, but act on it, which is compassion going out. In fact, the root of the word compassion is the same as the word compass and encompassment, suggesting that compassion encompasses all in its soul warming glow. Like the sun, which shines equally on all, compassion knows no discrimination or judgment but flows freely to all who find themselves within its radiating range.

Other qualities will respond in a similar manner. Think about a quality that you find attractive and then make some actions that embody it and you will soon realize that you have become its host. Then other people will also begin to recognize that quality as part of who you are and they will start expecting your behavior to reflect your connections to this chosen quality. Just try it and you might be surprised by the results you experience!

CHAPTER THREE

Quality Clusters

When you deliberately set out to invite a quality into your life and are successful, even to a small degree in doing so, you might become pleasantly surprised when the quality of your choosing becomes accompanied by other qualities. So, for example, you might target courage as a quality you wish to embody; then, having acted courageously, you might realize that you become stronger as well, with better stamina levels. All qualities—both positive and negative—have sisters and brothers, sons and daughters. So deception might be betrothed to lying and by the same token, charity can beget compassion or serenity can bring with it its big brother, peace.

Qualities can form whole strings of liaisons—by attracting one quality one can pull on a string that brings closer—into one's cognizance as well as one's energy field—other qualities that are related to it. Once a person becomes generous, for example, compassion or empathy or kindness will not be far behind. By the same token, one can meditate upon the quality of compassion, which will also cause a person to become more generous and giving.

Nothing is on its own and in seclusion. Qualities beget qualities, just as quality begets quality. It does not matter which quality one begins with—they are all connected and intertwined together. One can start the journey into the garden of qualities by connecting, for example, to gratitude. Calling over all the things one is grateful for on a daily basis can soon cause a person to connect to a feeling of serenity and peace. Once peace attends a person, it will bring with it a whole host of supporting qualities, like satisfaction, equanimity, tolerance, serenity, calm and patience, or any combination of these.

Qualities can be like a cluster of rare jewels that one wears in one's energy field. Without a word of reference to them others will feel their radiation and will want to be within their healing and calming influence. It is very telling when animals and young children cling to a person and "drink in" their calming radiation. When other people are attracted to a person's energy field because they want to feel their radiation, it does not take anything away from the person who has accumulated these beneficial qualities; it will enhance all who come into contact with them, providing they are open to sharing their energy and their time.

Saint Francis of Assisi, who collected around him people and animals alike who wanted to be within his radiating energy field, must have become host to a number of fine qualities which were attractive to humans and animals alike.

Our physical bodies are separate and contained within our skin, but our energetic bodies—our auras—intermingle and exchange frequencies all the time. When we stand in line at the bank, post office or store checkout, for example, we are taking in the energies of the person in front of us and the person behind, just as they are taking in ours. We also take in the energies of the checkout person or teller as we interact with them, even if they are sitting behind bullet proof glass in a bank. Sometimes we might not "feel like ourselves" or have thoughts that feel alien and different to our regular, habitual thoughts. It could be because we had spent a lot of time with other people and we are processing out their energy.

When you become a beacon of high qualities, expect

to become surrounded and celebrated by those who are attracted by those qualities and want to (consciously or unconsciously) bask in their presence and have their influence "rub off" onto them by contagion. If this happens, be glad, because by sharing your energies, you will attract more good qualities into your energy field.

CHAPTER FOUR

Acting the Part

*A*cting the part is adopting a behavior that connects to a quality. Just as reading about, say, an orange or even seeing a picture of it is very different to tasting it for yourself and holding it in your hand, so thinking or reading about a quality is very different to acting the part. Making an action that connects to a quality brings the frequency of that quality into one's energy field. Everyone's experience of a single quality might be unique, as we each bring to our exploration of any quality our individual experience, knowledge and education. One person's version of charity, for example, might feel totally inadequate to someone else. Or one person's expression of love might feel insincere to someone else who has a different idea of what love is.

Working with qualities is a free pursuit, yet most rewarding. As we connect to, for example, honesty or courage, we will become a little more honest or courageous ourselves and there will be a little more honesty or courage in the world for others to connect to. How do we do that? you might ask. Simply act in an honest or courageous way, and the essence of honesty or courage will accompany you and move through you as you do.

Ask anyone who speaks in public or performs as an artist about whether they had to overcome stage fright to be able to carry out their performance and they will no doubt tell you how they had to simply "fake it" before they were able to combat successfully their nervousness.

We have been given free will to be able to decide who and what we want to be. Once we make that decision, it

23

is then a question of creating a pathway from the desire to the reality and following its guidance. We can become whoever we want to be but it is up to us to act the part and to become fully the unique person we were meant to be. It is really down to us which qualities we embody in order to create for ourselves a life of quality!

Every time we perform an act expressing a specific quality, a little bit of the energy associated with that quality remains inside our energy field. For example, if you perform a courageous act, you will become a little more courageous and the quality of courage will begin to live with you and become part of your standard radiation and character formation. If you continue to act courageously (following our example of courage), eventually others will begin to see and recognize you as being courageous. They might even start seeking you out when they need courage themselves, because they feel it can "rub off" on them too. Qualities are contagious and once they become domiciled within a person's energy field, they can jump from person to person, just like a germ, and begin to germinate within their new environment, inspiring their new host to actions that previously might have been outside their comfort zone. If you spend time with a happy person, for example, will you not yourself feel happier and become uplifted? But beware, because by the same token, if you spend time with someone who is angry or disgruntled, you might become angry or disgruntled too!

If you want to have or be known for having a certain quality, the advice is simple: begin to act in a way that displays this quality. The first act might feel unfamiliar and out of character, but the next one will be easier and will feel a little bit more natural. Keep going and before you know it, you will become your chosen quality.

A friend of mine wanted to become more generous,

after having been told that he was cheap and stingy. For a whole month he deliberately set out to daily perform a generous act—he would give away one dollar to the first beggar he met. If he did not meet a beggar that day, he would tip the waiter at the restaurant beyond the 15% he previously had felt obliged to leave as a tip, or he would place his dollar in the jar on the counter of his favorite coffee shop. The entire exercise cost him a little over $30 but by the end of it he felt better about himself and his friends who witnessed his new behavior soon changed their view of him.

It might seem unimportant what other people think of us, especially people we know well, but they are custodians of an image of us as they see us, and we meet this image every time we see them. So if we can change how others see us, it will release us from our old habits and ways to enable us to reinvent ourselves more effectively and quicker. If you wish to embody a certain quality, it is important to take action with that quality in mind and, if possible, be witnessed while expressing it and radiating it into the world.

The real magic, however, happens when we have invited a quality into our life and it becomes part of our character. This is when we act with that quality without even thinking about it—it has become part of our makeup and the way we behave. This is when the new energy within our field radiates out on a permanent basis and other entities that are akin to it can respond and add to it. So, for example, if I become serene on a repetitive basis, eventually serenity will come and live within my energy field and people will begin to recognize me as a serene person. Then eventually, even in stressful and difficult situations, I will not get perturbed or rattled because serenity will be within my energy field, keeping me calm and centered.

A Garden of Qualities

Each quality we accumulate is a gift. Unlike material possessions, we can take these energy formations with us when we depart from this earthly realm. They can become our comfort while we are alive and our passport into a better tomorrow.

CHAPTER FIVE

Levels of Qualites

Qualities have many levels and as soon as a person explores and connects to one level of a particular quality, they will realize that there are more levels and deeper truths to feel and to know. Sometimes it is difficult to find the words to describe the feeling that might accompany a particular level of a specific quality, but the magic lies in the discovery of new territories and new revelations connected to each energetic level of a quality as it reveals its inner meanings and requirements.

Once a quality comes to live in one's energy field, it brings with it not only its requirement for maintenance and sustenance, but also its intelligence. For qualities do have their own intelligence which they will impart to their host, so they can be assured of continuance and longevity. Someone who becomes peaceful or humble will understand about peace or humility in ways that people who do not have these qualities do not understand. A person who connects to a new quality might even become surprised to find out that the quality they have invited into their life is not as they had anticipated. It probably has depths and aspects that the person had never even thought of before becoming its host.

When we check out the dictionary definition of a word describing a quality, we will find one, two or three meanings with quotes from literature and historical documents supporting and adding color to the definitions. This is a starting point but it is useful to remember that language is alive, evolving and changing all the time. A dictionary definition is like a snapshot of a moment in time; it is like a fossil, based on precedent and how the word describing that quality had been used in the past. However, as we progress we will need new words, phrases and descriptions to define new levels of qualities and higher energies, as we discover them and invite them into our life.

Every quality, although expressed with a single word, could probably have many words or phrases assigned to it to accurately describe its many levels. Take love, for example. Love means many different things to many different people."I love you" can mean such disparate things as "I like you," "I cherish you," "I desire you," or it can indicate a requirement for the other person to be or behave in a certain way. "Unconditional love" is a phrase that is often being used these days, but mostly the emotion it describes is far from unconditional. Love in its highest and purest form has indeed no conditions attached to it, but this is a very rare energy commodity indeed. To be a host to unconditional love one needs to become selfless and abandon the desire for personal gain within a relationship.

One can attempt to find words or phrases for the different levels of a particular quality. They might not be accurate descriptions of those levels of that quality, but the effort to search for and find the different notions associated with that quality will open up the perception and understanding that several energy levels do exist. Take peace, for example. At one level it might mean the absence of stress or strife, at another level it can mean the absence of war. At yet another level it might mean settlement to one's surroundings and living conditions. At yet another level it could mean the resolution to a quarrel or altercation. It can also mean the final rest a person experiences when they die, as in the phrase, "May he rest in peace."

Hope, as another example, is not just one energy, but a whole conglomerate of energies. It can be a wish for a better tomorrow on one end of the spectrum and an openness to change at the other. It can be a prayer or a demand, an invocation or an invitation.

The more levels and meanings we can identify within each quality we invite into our lives, the better chance we have of becoming energetically merged with those qualities. Understanding about the many levels of the energies we connect to will also allow us to develop and strengthen the qualities that have already taken up residence in our energy field.

At the lower end of the spectrum of seven levels of energy that exist on planet Earth, qualities are different and distinct, with their specific characteristics which are instantly recognizable and discernible. At the higher end of the spectrum, however, qualities become more similar as they begin to merge together reflect greater universal influences. At the highest level all qualities are an expression of universal love and are connected to the divine.

CHAPTER SIX

Virtues and Vices

*I*n olden days qualities were called virtues. If you add an *a* and shift the letters around to form an anagram, the word *virtues* becomes a *true visa*. Indeed, the act of connecting to a new quality allows a person to enter a new energy domain where that quality resides. Entering the field of peace, for example, is very different from thinking about peace, longing for peace or hoping for it. Within the field of a quality, longing for it ceases and one becomes it. One no longer longs for love because love is now in every breath and every moment of every day. One becomes love, one radiates love, one exudes love and other people will know it and feel it.

A person has a virtue when they become a virtuoso—a master, able to connect to a quality or qualities at will. When one masters a quality or an essence, one has access to it at any time. It is like the master piano player who can conjure up a melody at any time of day or night; once established, the virtue is always there. After many instances of connecting to a quality, it finally comes to reside in a person's energy field. It takes time and effort to build a quality into one's character formation. It might take years for a person to become patient, for example. But once the quality of patience is what they are and thus defines them, they will find it very difficult to behave in an impatient manner.

Virtues belong at the higher level of the energetic spectrum, while vices are lower energies which can become a threat to a person's wellbeing and are the antithesis to their higher qualities. As opposed to vices which hold a person in their grip and are addictive, virtues need to be wooed, sought after, won and assimilated into one's energy field.

The word qualities does not have an opposite—a word that would describe the energies that live at the lower end of the energetic spectrum. There is probably no better word than vices to describe these lower energetic forms, because it gives such a vivid description of how those energies work.

When a man or woman applies to join a monastery or a nunnery, they first become a novice. Being a novice means they are on trial to see if monastic life befits them and whether they have any vices. Only after this trial period, if it is established that they have no vices which could disrupt the secluded life of the monastery or nunnery, will they be invited to stay and join the order. From the standpoint of an energy understanding, a person does not have vices; it is the vice that has the person in its grip. Just like a carpenter's vice that holds two pieces of wood together while they are being glued, a vice is an energy that takes hold of a person's life. It will not let go until the person alters their behavior and frees themselves from the grip of that vice's energetic control.

Everything wants to continue to exist and needs to be fed to survive and grow. Both qualities and vices are energy formations which would wither and disappear if there were no human actions to provide them with new energy and to contribute to their continuance.

Qualities and vices cannot occupy the same space. That is why the best way to dispel the energies represented by vices is to superimpose them with new qualities. Inviting qualities into one's life can be a cure for many ailments and complaints. Take some of the deadly sins, for example. They all can be replaced by high energetic content: pride with humility, envy with warmth, wrath with patience or tolerance, greed with generosity, sloth with industriousness, lust with charity and gluttony with restraint. In medieval times the acronym SALIGIA was adopted to represent the seven deadly sins (derived from the first letters of the Latin words for the seven deadly sins: *superbia, avaritia, luxuria, invidia, gula, ira, acedia*—pride, greed, lust, envy, gluttony, wrath, sloth). It was believed that these seven sins give rise to all other vices.

Virtues were originally identified by the Greek philosophers Aristotle and Plato, who regarded temperance, wisdom, justice, and courage as the four most desirable character traits. After the New Testament was written, these four virtues became known as the cardinal virtues, while faith, hope and charity were referred to as the theological virtues.

A list of the seven heavenly virtues—to oppose the seven deadly sins—appeared later, in an epic poem entitled *Psychomachia*, or *Battle/Contest of the Soul*. Written by Aurelius Clemens Prudentius, a Christian governor, who died around 410 A.D., it describes the battle between good virtues and evil vices. The enormous popularity of this work in the Middle Ages helped to spread the concept of holy virtue throughout Europe. The seven virtues became identified as chastity, temperance, charity, diligence, patience, kindness and humility. Practicing them was said to protect one against temptation from the seven deadly sins, each one having its counterpart. Due to this, they are sometimes referred to as the "contrary virtues."

Today some of the words describing vices, such as sloth, wrath and gluttony, have fallen into disuse, but the energies they represent have not. Mostly referred to in modern times as laziness, anger and greed, these are energetic properties which still exist in the world and get added to every time a thought or action is committed associated with these vices. To combat these vices and win the battle for one's soul, the best way is to enter the garden of qualities and stake one's claim within its healing grounds.

The moment a quality is called into existence, its opposite is created as well. The planet Earth is a place of duality— for every action there is a reaction and for every virtue there is an opposing vice. If there was no impatience in the world, would we have a need for patience? Once patience was created, it became a cure for impatience, just as bravery is a cure for cowardice and generosity is a cure for greed.

Once attracted to a person's energy field, every quality will banish its opposite vice, just as every vice, once it takes up residence in a person's energy field, will exclude the opposite quality from their aura and life.

Building One's Character

*O*nce attracted into a person's energy field, qualities cause change and bring with them development that enhances a life, heals and creates new opportunities. A person who learns to be patient, for example (in the true sense of the word), will learn to better appreciate their surroundings as well as their relationships and ultimately they will value more their life and the experiences it offers. A person who deliberately sets out to spread warmth into the world will reap the rewards of their endeavors by collecting warmth and appreciation from others because warmth tends to be reciprocated with warmth.

This book is an attempt to understand the energies associated with different qualities and to help the reader connect to these sublime energies so they can benefit from their healing charge and appreciate their magnificence and the gifts they bring to anyone who endeavors to bask in their warming glow. It is not an attempt to exhaust the subject or even to provide accurate definitions or dissertations on the meanings of the various words used to describe the qualities we experience and connect to throughout our lives. It is an attempt to help the reader offer them a home so that there can be more quality in the world. This is something we can do to pay back for existence and make this world a better place.

This book is meant to help the reader become more aware of his or her energetic qualities and to set their feet upon the path of becoming more effective transformers and generators of quality energies.

A Garden of Qualities

Some qualities we acquire when young—we learn specific behaviors and attitudes from our parents, elders, teachers and mentors. Others we develop later in life, when we make friends, enter into intimate relationships or become parents ourselves. Others we might acquire while developing a career, pursuing a hobby or traveling to other cultures and distant lands. There is no bad time to connect to qualities—they are always available everywhere and await our relevant actions and appropriate attitude so they can become invited to accompany us on our journey through life. Qualities can become our armor, protecting us from negative energies and emotions.

The qualities we consciously choose to adopt and deliberately invite into our lives are more powerful than the virtues we inherited in a non-conscious, automatic way. The ones we consciously develop, with mindful intent and the power of our will providing the determination and power to help us succeed are guaranteed to last and accompany us throughout life's journey.

Once a person invites a quality into their life, they become its host. Just as one would do with any valued and welcomed visitor, it is then important to provide the facilities and circumstances within which that quality can flourish and grow.

So if one aspires to become a trustworthy person, for example, it will be important to act in a trustworthy manner, not once or twice, but on a continuous basis. To grow this quality within one's energy field, it will be essential to keep one's word, keep one's appointments, keep secrets one has been entrusted with and to not promise too much. The origin of becoming untrustworthy is often not the deliberate intention to disappoint or a sloppy attitude. Quite the opposite; it is often the desire to please that is the root of becoming untrustworthy. So learning to better manage one's time might be the fastest route to becoming a trustworthy person. Once this task has been successfully accomplished, it will make room for other qualities to accompany trustworthiness in one's energy field, such as honesty and reliability. When there is no need for excuses or lies to cover up an unfulfilled promise, a space is created for new essences and qualities to enter one's energy field. Thus to become energetically tidy and frugal is the fastest way to create space for new qualities within one's garden of qualities.

Once one embodies a certain essence or, in other words, when it comes to reside in one's energy field, it will go wherever the person goes and will radiate around them. A serene person, for example, settled to who they are and grateful for their lot, will radiate serenity and gratitude wherever they go and whatever they do. So on entering a room a serene person will influence the room's energy, as will a compassionate person or indeed an angry person. Every person radiates into their home, their place of work and into the district, the country and ultimately the world and the universe. When a serene person enters a room, they can even cause arguments to cease, because in the presence of serenity an argument might suddenly appear petty and pointless by the people involved in the altercation. Therefore, whatever qualities you radiate are affecting the people you live with as well as all those you meet on a daily basis, whether at work, or out and about when shopping, eating at a restaurant or simply walking down the street.

In one's pursuit of selflessness, it might be a good idea to come at the question—what qualities would you want to embody?—from a worldview standpoint rather than a local personal view. So the question to ask is, what qualities does the world need? And if the answer is, for example, peace, then to help the energy of the world one would need to find ways to increase peace in one's life, perhaps by spending ten or twenty minutes each day in contemplation or meditation about peace.

Qualities mark the difference between an ordinary person and an extraordinary person. Having a quality is like having a garden and tending to one's plants—you need to plant the seeds, nourish the soil, water and fertilize the plants and make sure they have everything they need to grow. So once you decide to grow a quality—say, courage—one way to do so is to develop a practice to bring it into your energy field. You could, for example, regularly imagine yourself behaving courageously, especially in difficult circumstances which might require you to be courageous. Then when such a circumstance arises, it will be easier to connect to the quality of courage and invite it into your life.

CHAPTER EIGHT

Exercises and Meditations

1. Exercise

Choose seven qualities you would wish to embody in your life. Then for each quality think of an action that in your mind expresses that quality. Plan to perform each of these actions daily for a full lunar month (28 days). This does not necessarily mean performing seven actions every day for a month; you can choose one, two or three actions during the first month, one or two during the second and so on.

Twenty-eight days is a lunar cycle—this is how long your skin cells live and this is also the monthly cycle of the womb. It is the first level of establishment—it takes 28 days for a quality to begin to become embedded in your energy field. The next level of establishment is a planetary cycle—28 seasons, or seven years. The third level is a Saturnian cycle which is 28 years. Once something has been established in one's energy field for 28 years, it will be almost impossible to shift. If it is of a high quality, why would you want to?

2. Exercise

What qualities do you radiate into the world? Do you deliberately bring them with you when you go to work or to meet another person? What can be said of your home or your room? What qualities live there? What about your car? If you find these questions difficult, ask someone else who knows you what they think. What do they feel when they enter your home or your room or when they get into your car? Once you know what qualities represent your strengths, you can deliberately set about enhancing and adding to those qualities.

3. Exercise

Imagine a closet full of qualities. What qualities would you like to be there? Not qualities you want to receive, but qualities you would want to have access to. We all might want more love in our life, for example, but do we have it to give, to radiate, to spread it around? When you wake up, imagine opening your closet of qualities and choosing two or three that you plan to radiate into the world that day.

4. Qualities Meditation

This meditation is designed to help you acquire a quality that you need or feel you want more of.

Find a quiet place where you will not be disturbed for ten or fifteen minutes. Make sure your cell phone is off.

Take a few deep breaths. Breathe in and out, in and out, in and out.

Now think of a quality you would like to have or that you feel you need more of. It could be anything— for example, patience, strength, persistence, compassion, generosity... the list is endless. Take a few moments to contemplate this. If you feel you need more than one quality, then that is fine too. But try to limit it to two or three at most. You can always do this meditation again and choose a different quality.

Now that you have chosen your quality or qualities, think of a definition—what this quality means to you. There is no right or wrong definition because it is simply to express your understanding of this quality at this time.

Now imagine a shield—it could be round, rectangular or heart shaped—any shape you like. It can be made of metal, wood, leather, plastic or a combination of materials.

Now think of an image that would best represent your quality or qualities. For example, an oak tree for strength, a pyramid for endurance, a cheetah for speed, a rose for finesse. It can be anything—animal, vegetable, mineral, human, symbol. Take a moment to think about this.

Now that you have your symbol, or image, place it on your shield. It can be painted or chiseled or glued on.

Now imagine that you are picking up your shield. This shield can protect you against everything that is opposite to your quality. Mentally name a few emotions or behaviors that are anti-thesis to your quality. As you do so, lift your shield up to protect yourself from them. So, for example, if your quality was patience, you now have a protection against impatience. Strength will shield you from weakness, diligence from procrastination and so on.

So now remember your image and this shield that is now part of your arsenal and toolkit. You can pick it up whenever you feel the need.

To finish the meditation, the final step is to try and refine your initial definition, by adding your new understanding and experience about your chosen quality. Do not refer back to the initial definition but start over, defining anew your chosen quality.

Take a few deep breaths—in and out, in and out, in and out. Open your eyes and feel refreshed.

5. Friends Meditation

This meditation is aimed at getting to know yourself better and recognizing your strengths.

Find a quiet place where you will not be disturbed for twenty minutes or so. Make sure your cell phone is off. Close you eyes.

Take a few deep breaths. Breathe in and out, in and

out, in and out.

Picture five of your best friends or people who are close to you and whose company you enjoy. It can be family members, your partner, colleagues at work; people you spend time with and whom you respect. Take a moment to think who these five people are. One way to think of it is to ask yourself—if you were stranded on a desert island, who would you want to be there with you, not from the standpoint of their skills, like boat building or growing food, but from the standpoint of sharing their company and spending time with them.

Think of the first person. Picture their face, their smile, their posture. Imagine they are standing in front of you. Shake their hand or give them a hug; whichever feels more comfortable for you to do.

Now stand back a pace and ask yourself, what is their most endearing quality or qualities; what do you admire most about this person? Take a moment to do this.

Now you have identified this quality (or qualities), tell this person you are looking at that you admire this quality about them and if possible, explain why. You can give an example or examples from your experience with this person, or something you read about or know about this person, telling them how and when and why you had observed them manifesting this quality. You can speak to them mentally, in your mind, or speak softly or out loud— whatever you feel comfortable with.

Now imagine that you are taking that quality or qualities into yourself from the other person. They are willingly offering you this quality, because they have a lot of it to give.

And now they are saying to you that you have this quality or qualities as well because you would not have been able to recognize it in another person if you did not have it yourself. Imagine that now.

Now confirm this by admitting to them that yes, indeed you do have this quality or qualities as well.

Thank this person and say goodbye as they disappear into the distance or walk away. Imagine this now.

Repeat this process with each of the five people you have chosen.

Now try to remember all five (or more) qualities you have admitted to having. Repeat them quietly to yourself, saying "I am patient, strong,," or whatever… Spend a moment thinking about each of these qualities.

Slowly open your eyes and feel well. You might want to take a moment and write down the qualities your friends had shared with you, so you can remember and strengthen them during the days and weeks to come.

6. Exercise: In the Manner of the Quality

This exercise is designed for a group of people and helps the participants find multiple ways to express various qualities.

One person leaves the room, while the others decide what quality they would like to work with. The first person is invited back into the room and asks the group to make various actions "in the manner of the quality." They then guess what the chosen quality is.

For example, the group chooses the word "care." Person A comes into the room and asks one of the group (person B) to "Pass me a mug in the manner of the word." Person B cleans the table and puts a cup holder in place before settling the mug in front of person A. Person A then either asks for another action to be performed or guesses the quality.

7. Future You Meditation

Imagine you at 10, 20, 30, 40, up to the age you currently are. Try to find a word or phrase to describe how you were at each age. Note the changes and development as you progressed through the years.

Project yourself into the future—to the next decade and beyond.

Imagine yourself in the future and surround that image of the future you with the qualities you would like to have as you reach your forthcoming ages.

Part Two

A Garden of Qualities

Care

*A caring person extends their energy and consideration
with discernment, to include others within their energy field.*

CHAPTER ONE

Care

C are is both a verb and a noun. As a verb it speaks of a commitment, an emotional involvement. Who and what do you care about? Care is a valuable property and you do not want to waste it by caring for people, situations and things that do not matter.

What about possessions? Do you care if you lose something valuable? If you do, do you have ways to get over it and move on? Caring about something lost or the past can be a futile exercise, because you cannot bring the past back. So have a care about the present moment and plant within this moment the seeds of how you wish to become tomorrow.

If you care about someone, it suggests you have feelings for them, you like them and you include them in your energetic "circle of warmth." Your energetic circle of warmth are people you think well of, the people you send warmth to when you think of them, the people you care about. You wish these people well and you are interested in their well-being, even if you are at distance from them.

As a noun care appears in such sayings as "take care," "having care" or being a "care-giver." It suggests care is like a commodity which can be taken and given away. When we say to someone, "Take care," when, for example, they are going out onto an icy street, we mean to suggest that they should be careful, which speaks of being mind-full and with due attention, being in the now, being watchful and not rash, fast or care-less. In this instance care is the energy of attention and mindfulness which we can switch on or ignore at our peril.

When you put the two aspects of care together—the verb and the noun—it suggests that care combines both a mental and emotional connection to other people or things. We can care about our house, our car or any other possessions we might have. "I really cared about that vase," we might say after someone has inadvertently smashed it to smithereens, "it belonged to my late mother." This would indicate that by reflection, the object was connected to a person who belonged to our energetic circle of warmth.

The quality of care goes beyond the idea of caring for something or someone. Care as a quality talks about having an openness and compassion to the suffering of others. Care is usually accompanied by a sensitivity to the feelings and responses of others. We are not alone. Care is an energetic thread that connects us to other people, the environment, our surroundings and, of course, ourselves. "She takes great care about her appearance," someone might say about another person. It means it matters to her how she appears to others. But one could also ask, does she take the same care about her mind, her spirit and the people she deals with?

How much care do you take about what you surround yourself with? Look at the place where you sleep. Is it cluttered? Do you have some old papers lying around, or things that are no longer relevant to your life? We are constantly changing, so the clothes, objects we possess, things we say and do should reflect those changes. That way you can keep the energy you surround yourself with fresh and freely flowing.

If you take care of someone—say, you are a caregiver—you will take into account their needs and adjust their diet, for example, to their current state of health. Taking care of oneself is trying, to the best of one's ability, to be up to date with your own needs and requirements. If you are on a spiritual journey, your needs will constantly change as you require finer and finer energy food. So you need to find a supply of that energy food and find a source where it can be obtained. Where can you get more care from? From those who have it—for example, you can study the lives of those who have demonstrated care, like Jesus Christ, Mahatma Gandhi, Mother Teresa, the Dalai Lama, St. Francis of Assisi or characters from literature, like Robin Hood or even Superman.

If you want to have more care in your life, it is important to get a sense of the quality of care—what is it associated with, where does it come from, how does it manifest, what is the root of its cause? People who care are summoned to action—they are motivated by the need for change. If all were well with the world, maybe we would not need so much care.

If you make a suggestion at work—say, how to improve the filing system or why the purchase of a better computer should save money in the long term—you are demonstrating that you care. Any improvement that you introduce into your life or into the life of others or into the environment is a sign that you care.

So sometimes, if you want more care in your life, it can work the other way round: introduce an improvement into your home or at work, into your diet or your wardrobe, and perhaps a little bit more of the frequency of care will come and live in your energy field. If it does, it will emanate from you, illuminating the edge of your aura as care reaches out to others and inspires them by contagion to care more for themselves and their health, their life, their surroundings and their environment.

Here is an important consideration: do you care what

other people think? Some people waste a lot of energy caring and agonizing over what others think. Of course, it is important what other people think because other people do influence your life—they can employ you, fire you, go out with you or dis you, marry you or divorce you. However, what other people think is always a secondary consideration because the first consideration has to be what you think about you. If you think well of yourself, if you value and respect yourself, then others will appreciate you more as well and learn to see you as you see yourself. You should care what you think of yourself and work to earn your self-respect.

So on the one hand we should not care what others think and on the other we should care deeply what others think. What others think adds power to what we do and who we are. That is why the one common ingredient to all rights of passage ceremonies is the fact that they are witnessed. By watching someone getting married, for example, the guests are adding their energetic power to the ceremony.

One should care about what those who one cares about think, because they are one's support system, energetically speaking. These are the people who will hold in custodianship our actions which they have witnessed and the exchanges between us. Those shared experiences are energetically written into the energy field between us and the people who have witnessed us throughout our life. But when pursuing a goal and having made up our mind to do something, or be something, it is important not to care what others think because sometimes people, even those who wish us well and who we care about, can think of all kinds of impediments and reasons why we should not pursue our chosen path or aim. So caring what other people think is not necessarily a bad thing—you can learn from other people's criticisms and reflections. But if it stops you in your purpose, it most definitely can be detrimental to your life.

If we want to increase the quality of care into our life, there are several ways we can do it. One is to deliberately and consciously increase our energetic circle of warmth by adding new people into its warming glow. Choose someone you know and decide that when you think of them you will think with warmth and send them good energy. You will not judge them or envy them; you will not second-guess their actions or think you know better what they should be doing with their life. You will energetically let them be as they are and be glad they exist in the world.

Another way to increase care in your life is to add care to your daily activities, even to mundane, everyday actions. Take, for example, the act of making a cup of tea or cooking a meal. You can add care to this simple act by being mindful about the person you are making it for (including yourself). You can think well of that person as you pour water into the mug or place a pot on the stove, and add a little bit of love, warmth and encouragement into the hot liquid or the dish you are making. See if they (or you) can taste the difference. Experiments by Dr. Masaru Emoto, described in his book, *Messages From Water*, have shown that water retains our thoughts and feelings. Food does as well. Ancient Egyptians would charge their food before consuming it. There are many peoples around the world, including Christians, who pray before meals. It causes a person to remind themselves to be grateful for the gifts they receive and to include those gifts in their energetic circle of warmth. A prayer said over the food will energetically charge it, transforming it into a more wholesome meal. If you don't believe me, take two plates of any dish and say a prayer over one of them, ignoring the other. Now taste both and see if you can tell the difference.

If a child cares for a wounded animal, for example, like a bird with a broken wing, he or she is inviting care into their life. It will be much easier for him or her to have care later on in life if they do so. We often learn to assimilate qualities early on in life, as we learn from parents, friends, teachers and mentors. But it is never too late to start and to decide to bring new virtues into your life. One of the best ways to teach a child to have care is to encourage them to be responsible for looking after an animal or for planting a tree and watching it grow. Taking care of an animal is learning what it needs, not what we might think it needs.

Sometimes a person can care too much. They get easily upset by the news or by what other people say to them. These sensitive souls seem to "carry the cares of the world" on their shoulders. The other extreme is not caring, when experiences or information is like "water off a duck's back." Somewhere in the middle is where you want to be. Have care with discernment.

We care according to our priorities. If we want to have control about who and what we care about, we need to know our priorities and work to reinforce them. If, for example, I care about my health, I will exercise regularly and research what foods are good for me. If I care about my job, I will be punctual and conscientious at work. If I care about my partner, I will be aware of his or her needs and dedicate time, effort and finances to help him/her fulfill them.

There is a difference between a careless person and a carefree person. The word careless has a pejorative sense to it and it describes someone who lacks care to the point of making mistakes, dropping things and generally making a mess of things. Carefree, on the other hand, brings with it images of release and getting rid of cares that might be constricting and limiting a person's freedom of action. These two words indicate that too much care or too many cares can be a hindrance, while lack of care can cause a person to be less effective in one's endeavors. It is therefore for each person to find the balance between the two, providing, of course, they care to try it.

Where can you find care? One place where it lives is in the idea of motherhood. When thinking of motherhood and what a mother is, and how she cares for her children, as any mother of any species cares for her young, one thinks of her caring moments, like how she looks after a sick child or how she wants her children to be happy. A mother is an embodiment of caring parenthood. Of course, there are uncaring mothers, too, but here we are referring to the archetype of mother and the nurturing essence of maternity. A father cares for his children too, but his archetype cares in a different way. Less hands-on, but more in the sense of foraging and working out in the world for the good of the family.

How do you know what or who a person cares about? Look to see what they spend their time on—that will give you the answer. How do you stop caring for someone? By no longer giving them your time, your energy and your care.

The greatest gift you can give someone is your time and your energy. If you visit a sick friend in hospital, the best way you can give them your energy is by holding their hand and consciously sending energy through your hands into theirs. If you bring them flowers, realize that energy flows through flowers into the stems. You can therefore ask the patient to hold the stems of the flowers, while you direct your energy from your hands into the flowers.

A Garden of Qualities

In this manner, the flowers become funnels channeling energy from you to the patient who needs it for their convalescence.

To increase the energy of care you surround yourself with, pay attention to details—keep your surroundings clean and fresh. Try not to care about small things that do not matter (as recommended by Richard Carlson in his book *Don't Sweat the Small Stuff*). But care about now, this moment in time, which is the only time when you can improve your life and make changes for the better. It is now and only now that you can invite new qualities into your energetic garden of qualities. When you change something in your life (it can be a hairdo or it can be something more dramatic, like a new partner or a new job), it shows that you care (about your looks or your life).

To understand better abut the quality of care, look to those who have cared. History is full of people who cared about the environment or about fairness and were prepared to risk their own lives to fight for what they felt was right. These are people who cared in a big way and we can learn from their stories about many qualities (not only care), such as dedication, determination and love.

Be based in your core and care will accompany you.

Exercise

1. Who do you care about? Write down the names of five people you care about.

2. What do you care about? Write down five things you care about.

3. What are the confirming actions to show that you care? Find ten things you can do to demonstrate your care for each of the items on your list (one for each).

Group Exercise

If you were playing "In the Manner of the Word," as described in Part One, Chapter Eight, and the quality that needed to be portrayed was care, when asked "Pass me the mug in the manner of the word," one could wipe the table before putting the mug down, or bring a coaster to protect the table from the heat. Then the person portraying care could say, "Careful, it's hot."

Meditation

Imagine sitting around a fire somewhere in nature like in a clearing in a forest at night. Imagine all the people you care about sitting around the fire with you—your family, your friends, people you used to know and liked, anybody you have a warm feeling for. Now imagine inviting into the circle of people sitting around the fire someone whom you might have just met and like, or someone that you used to know who now is at distance from you. Invite them into your circle of warmth and tell them why you want them to be part of the gathering.

CARE

At first care is the presence of mind;
Be careful means being watchful and slow
Then having care is to others being kind
Giving them what they need
so they can flourish and grow.
Not caring means I don't mind;
Care adds importance to an action or deed
Attention to detail is its sign
So it can grow from a very small seed
Into behavior that is considerate and fine.
Care for oneself is the next symptom of care
Valuing one's life and one's time,
Being grateful for earth, water, fire and air
Appreciating all that is sublime.
Then care grows and radiates with a touch
It extends to all within one's sphere;
Even a look can say, "I care very much"
Whether you are far away or near.

Belief

*Belief allows a person to penetrate into
the unseen and unknown.*

CHAPTER TWO

Belief

O nly humans have beliefs. One of the reasons we have belief is because so much of what is around us is hidden. We are always facing the veil between what is seen and what is unseen, what is known and what is unknown, between the present and the future. Belief can be a substitute for knowledge. A religious person will believe in God, whereas an atheist believes that there is no God; they both have their beliefs.

So we penetrate into the unknown with our belief, and each person develops their own belief system based on tradition, religion, experience and research. Belief of itself is not a quality that stands on its own; it is always associated with something else—the object of our belief. "I believe in angels," a person might say (or sing), or "I believe in you," or "I believe you." Belief can be a conduit along which information may flow. If we do not believe in something or we do not believe what someone is telling us, we block that particular passageway and do not accept the information that is offered to us. "I don't believe it," we will say and perhaps think no more about it.

Events that have happened in the past are presented to us as history and stories. We might believe them to be true, but we have no way of checking them out, unless we do the research ourselves and examine old records and documents, and rummage through libraries and Internet sites. Was Richard the Third the villain Shakespeare had portrayed him to be and was he responsible for the death of the princes in the tower? We might believe another point of view, but will we ever really know? We believe that there was an American War of Independence or a French Revolution and a storming of the Bastille. We have read about these events in our history books, though we had not witnessed them ourselves and most of us have not seen the relevant documents that would prove these facts with our own eyes. But belief allows us to accept as real events that we had no way of witnessing ourselves. This is the known unknown.

The reason I mention history is because having been brought up in Poland during the communist era, the history I was taught was biased and in many cases not true at all. So even when learning about accepted historical facts, they can still be presented with a biased or one-sided viewpoint.

Does an attorney believe his or her client when the accused proclaims his innocence? Does he go along with his client's version of the events? If he does not believe his client is not guilty, what does he base his conviction on? When a jury sums up the evidence, sometimes, if not everyone agrees—some will believe the defense and others will side with the prosecution. Why? And how is belief connected with feelings and instincts?

When do we realize that not everything we hear is the truth? How old are we when this realization dawns on us? Perhaps we might come to the conclusion that even school history books sometimes lie, when we read about the history of our country and later find out that the stories described had been altered for the sake of political propaganda and convenience. When do we learn to lie ourselves and hide the truth if, for example, we want to stay home from school because we had not done our homework? "Mommy, I am not feeling well," we might say, and she will ask, "What is wrong?" "My tummy hurts," we say with a moan and she believes us because to her knowledge we had never lied before. Now she is concerned and we feel bad that we have deceived her, but we persevere in our deception, insisting that the lie is the truth.

Belief is a powerful tool because it is a lance into the future and into the past—it penetrates beyond the veil into territories that are otherwise inaccessible to us. It allows us to access the unknown with our imagination.

As far as belief is concerned, there are two extreme attitudes one can adopt—one is the cynic who does not believe anything he is told and the other is the gullible person who believes and trusts other people too easily, and is easily deceived.

Throughout our lives we choose our beliefs and adjust them according to our experiences in the world and with other people. Some we acquire while growing up; others we adopt when we learn to think for ourselves and question our parents' beliefs. Our beliefs change and evolve as we live; they are an inherent part of a life's journey. They can bring hope and comfort and the settlement that life is not in vain.

Can you imagine nature having the need for belief and disbelief or animals lying to each other? It is preposterous to even think of such a possibility. Imagine a bee that had discovered a field of flowers overflowing with sweet nectar. He comes back to the hive and does his little dance that bees do, to inform the other bees of his find. But this bee decides to keep the newly discovered information to himself, so he does a deceptive dance indicating that the flowers can be found in the opposite direction to their real location. So all the bees, who believe in the information given to them, set out in the wrong direction in search of sustenance and pollen. What a laughable example! No—animals and nature do not lie; they respond to what is in the present.

A Garden of Qualities

Belief has only two states—it is either present or absent. It can be a highway to higher states of being. If you believe there are spiritual entities and angelic beings, you can connect to their levels, or at least attempt to do so. Without belief, the entrance to higher realms is cut off and no attempt to connect to them is made, unless a person is prepared to suspend their disbelief.

One day my husband and I were demonstrating to a group of people how to see the energy around a person's body. There was a man in the audience who saw the energetic field or aura around a person for the first time in his life. He was amazed and after the demonstration he asked if he could purchase the light bulb that allowed him to see such a phenomenon. He was not prepared to believe that he could see energy with his own eyes, despite the evidence of his sense of sight! Of course, we insisted that the bulb was just an ordinary bulb, but the man did not believe us and went away thinking that we wanted to keep the secret of "aura seeing light fixture" to ourselves.

The opposite of belief is doubt. Sometimes human experiences cause a person to doubt their beliefs. The author's landlady, born in Slovakia into a Jewish family was incarcerated in the notorious Auschwitz concentration camp as a young girl during World War Two. She often says that her religious beliefs were challenged when she witnessed atrocities committed against children. Sometimes she would wonder if there really was a God and if there was, why would He allow such crimes to be committed.

Belief is a glue that brings people together who share the same beliefs—whether tribal, religious or even superstitious. Belief is the breath of life, for without belief there is no hope. We are meant to have belief and to reach beyond the veil into that which is hidden, occulted and ineffable.

"I believe in life after death" is a very different statement to the assertion, "I am certain there is life after death." The latter implies utter conviction, based on research and perhaps even a near death experience or some other acceptable evidence. "I believe in life after death" opens the door to further investigation, to wondering about what really happens after we die and possibly to preparation for our physical demise and further spiritual journey. But a person who does not believe in life after death is closed to the possibility and therefore might miss the opportunity to connect to all the marvelous images, ideas and hopes associated with a new life after this one. Therefore belief is also the gateway to hope and several other qualities, such as forgiveness, reconciliation and love that with belief can find an entry port into human affairs.

The more others believe in us, the more we are able to believe in ourselves. This also works the other way around: the more we believe in ourselves, the more others will come to believe in us also. Believing in a person's ability gives them the confidence to believe in themselves. "I believe in you" does not mean that we believe in another person's existence, but we believe in their ability to succeed in whatever it is that they choose to do.

Belief in the future is associated with hope. Belief in anything says we think it exists, so believing in the future assumes there is one. Belief treads the fine line between hope and assumption—it can be reasonable or unreasonable. As we know from some amazing stories of healing, even seemingly unreasonable belief can bring positive results. So there is a sense that belief needs to be bold and imaginative in order to break through barriers of stagnation and bigotry. However, we also need to remember that there are inherent dangers in blind belief, fanatical belief or unreasoned belief. Therefore, according to the author a very useful stance to have is to question everything and make decisions based on common sense, research and unbridled optimism.

Proof is what transforms belief into certainty. A scientist might believe in a theory, but once proven, the theory becomes an accepted fact. There are of course theories and theologies that cannot be proven, so their very existence depends on continued belief. In his book titled *Proof of Heaven,* the neurosurgeon, Eben Alexander describes his near-death experience following a severe case of meningitis during which he was diagnosed as being brain dead. For him this experience was proof enough that heaven exists. However, not all his readers will agree that one man's visit to heaven while lying in a coma is proof enough.

Throughout our lifetime questions arise challenging our beliefs. A person who has experienced trauma or has witnessed war atrocities might question their beliefs in a benevolent god or a friendly universe. Each person develops their own belief system throughout their lifetime. Often those beliefs change and develop as the person goes through new experiences and learns to trust (or distrust) the evidence of their senses.

"Seeing is believing" is a known adage. However, there will always be unanswered questions that reach beyond the evidence of our senses. There will always be the need to employ belief to venture into the realms of the unknown unknown. This is where belief is such a powerful tool.

Belief in oneself is perhaps the most important form of belief a person can have. It gives one strength and the willingness to go on. It allows one to reach beyond one's current status and abilities towards the future, believing that one has the potential to grow and develop. Belief in self is contagious. If we can radiate the quality of belief, others will respond by seeing the potential we truly believe we have. If we do not believe in ourselves, why should anyone?

The study of human genetics assures us of our development as a specie. We are at a point in human evolution where our beliefs are challenged: is the evolutionary journey complete or do we believe we are still evolving and could become super-humans if we were able to access the dormant 90% of our brains?

Religion and faith are based on the premise that there is an unknown unknown. There are many legends and beliefs to be found in literature and lore around the world describing the origin of creation and our human species. Where did we come from? Where are we going? These are the mysteries of life that we hold dear. We learn to settle to the fact that we do not know. Belief calls for tolerance and understanding because every person is entitled to their beliefs, no matter how outlandish they may seem to another person. One of the rich aspects of the world is the fact that there are different beliefs around the world. Different nations and peoples believe in a variety of deities, gods and spirits; they have their unique stories and beliefs.

We have inherited a rich treasure of recorded beliefs—it is for each person to choose their own and create their unique belief system that will sustain them throughout life and perhaps even beyond.

BELIEF

In the absence of knowledge there is a belief
That allows us to look behind the veil
If we tread lightly, like a deer or a thief
We can enter the realms
that lie behind what we know well.
Belief is a lance that penetrates the past
And to the future opens up the door
It allows us to glance beyond the die that are cast
Into legends and myths and lore.

BELIEF (2)

At first I believe everything I am told
All the news I hear and stories of old;
Then with discernment I question what I hear,
I learn to check facts and ask without fear.
Then I assemble a belief system that works for me
Based on what I know for sure,
what I experience and see.
But then there are answers
I cannot prove throughout—
Some I will accept but some still cause doubt.
Belief allows me to reach behind the curtain
To ask questions and keep searching
until I can be certain.

Respect

Respect is to look again and
does not assume that everything stays the same
from one moment to the next.

CHAPTER THREE

Respect

Respect means to look again—as in *spectare*—to see/look in Latin, and in such words as spectacle, spectators and spectacles (glasses). It means not only to look again but also to think again or rethink. It is a bulwark against familiarity. It is to look again, as if for the first time, at people we know, places we frequent and situations we are participant in.

Familiarity breeds contempt is the saying. The root of the word familiarity is the same as in the word family. Our family are the people we are most familiar with, even though they are the closest to us and care for us the most. We tend to take our family for granted. One way to respect our nearest and dearest who are our family is to deliberately increase our respect for them; in other words, to look at them in a new light.

"Know thyself," the oracle at the Temple of Apollo at Delphi suggested, as do all esoteric traditions and personal development gurus. How can we increase our self-knowledge as well as our self-respect? One way is to frequently ask the questions, "How have I changed over the last year or so? Am I a better person? If so, in what way? What qualities have I been developing?" Can you describe the new you and identify the qualities and strengths you now have? Or do you think of yourself in old, familiar ways?

Realize that by developing new qualities, not only are you a better person, but you are radiating those qualities into the world, the district, the home and in all situations you find yourself in.

It is interesting that we "pay our respects" rather than

give them. This implies that respect is a due or a fee. It also suggests it is an energetic currency. Perhaps it means that respect needs to be first earned for us to be able to pay it.

Young people are often told to have respect for their elders—teachers, mentors and parents. Then later in life they might realize that that respect was not necessarily warranted. It is almost as though the child is required to pay with the currency of respect to every adult they meet, but not so much respect is necessarily offered in return to the child. Those who do offer respect to a child acknowledge the child's individuality and their entitlement to their own unique thoughts and feelings. Those grown-ups who pay respect to children will reap the rewards of curious and unusual conversations. Children think in unconventional ways and the innocent mind of a child can be an inspiration to someone who is now an adult and is open to listen. The respect between these two—the child and the grown-up—can flow both ways, offering insights and learning to both.

Two people who have a respect for each other will benefit from knowing each other. Respect is an energy that allows for more in-depth dealings—it ascertains that nothing needs to be proven. It is like an electrical conductor, within which good energy flows both ways. When there is no respect, invariably a person feels the need to prove their worth; lack of respect makes a person feel at less.

A person can cause respect by being unpredictable and by being willing to change. It will make a witness or associate take another look, to see who they are dealing with today. Habitual behavior can become the antithesis of respect; it can lead to familiarity and assumption. Habitual acts dull the senses because we become used to them and begin to expect them from someone whose habits we have witnessed over time. People who are in a relationship for a long time learn to anticipate the other person's moods, feelings, reactions and even their verbal responses. There is a great comfort in knowing another person so well, but it can also lead to the diminishment of respect. It all depends on the underlying sentiment that has been built up between partners.

Respect does not allow a person to take another for granted. In fact, a respectful person will not take anything for granted—their family, their home, their relationship or anything else that is sharing their life. They know that everything they have can easily be taken away and they appreciate what is theirs while it lasts. So one way to encourage respect into one's energy field is through gratitude. These two qualities—respect and gratitude— can often be found together in a person's attitude towards their family, friends and life circumstances.

People sometimes expect or demand respect from others, especially if they are in a position of power or leadership. But like trust, real respect has to be earned. It is a person's behavior that forges respect, so developing qualities in one's garden of qualities is the fastest way to earn respect. If you surprise the people you know with your integrity, honesty, punctuality, warmth, generosity and many others from a million of possible qualities, energetically you will become regal, surrounded by the incandescent radiation of someone who silently commands respect without ever having to ask for it.

RESPECT

At first we respect elders
because we are told that we should;
They are our teachers and mentors
and "it's for our own good."
Later respect is a recognition of worth,
It is earned by merit and not given at birth.
We respect the evidence of actions,
achievements and deeds—
The artist, performer and the guide who leads;
Then we learn to respect the life that is our own—
Here for a few short years, a body on loan.
Then we respect time as we watch it diminish
We spend it with care
because we know its supply will finish.
Finally we respect life wherever it appears
All life is sacred we learn through our years.

Meditation

Take a moment to think of one member of your family. Consider that this person is not "the same old …" (fill in the name) you knew last year, two years ago or even yesterday. They are changing, evolving and aging every day, just as you are. Take a minute to consider these changes and perhaps find a few words to describe this person and to identify the changes that have been occurring in them over the last months or years.

Hope

*Hope reaches toward the future with
optimism and a feeling that the best outcome
is always possible.*

CHAPTER FOUR

Hope

*H*ope is the human ability to envision a positive result in any situation where the outcome is still unknown.

Mostly when we think of hope, we think of the future, as in, "I hope you get better soon," "I hope they give me the job/promotion," "I hope he asks me out." But it can also refer to the past, as in, "I hope it turns out that it was not my son who broke the classroom window." So hope can apply to anything where we don't have certainty about its outcome, whether the past, present or future. "I hope to win," we might say.

"High hopes" suggests there are levels to hope. The saying usually refers to a person's promising future. Nobody, however, says, "low hopes." Perhaps there are degrees of hope, depending on the probability of the event that is hoped for happening. Or perhaps there are levels of hope depending on the significance of the event in question. "I hope it doesn't rain tomorrow" is one level of hope; "I hope he asks me to marry him" is quite another.

In Polish there is a saying that hope is the mother of the stupid, indicating that hope is not necessarily anchored in reality and can deceive a person into harboring false hopes. But without hope we would all become despondent and depressed. So perhaps to hope is not such a stupid thing to do after all. Hope is also the mother of the optimist and the believer. If you can envision something, it can happen. Hope allows a person to create images in one's mind. Images formed by the imagination have an energetic component and depending on the strength of a person's hope, these images can become their future reality.

It has been said that for an illumined man to think it is to create it. An illumined man (or woman) will add potency and action to the imagery to make their vision come true and will meditate to reinforce his (or her) projection into the future. In the mouths and minds of the uninitiated, hope is nothing more than a wish. But in the mouth, mind and heart of the developed person, it is a lance of power. Hope is an important component in the Law of Attraction working—it is an attraction or a beam of power energetically sent towards a target with the intention of bringing that target closer to home and making it become a reality. Rather than being an ethereal, unreal concept, in the realms of energy hope is a very practical discipline. In practicing hope, one can indeed make one's dreams come true.

With development hope becomes a lance of power, rather than an empty phrase. When saying, "I hope you get better soon," one can send one's energy with a petition to the healing powers, which can help another person get better sooner. When using one's power this way it is important not to hope to the detriment of another person or group. So to say, "I hope you win" is to hope someone else loses. Best to say and think, "I hope the best man/woman/player wins."

Hope can help a person in difficult times. It suggests change is possible. No matter how difficult a situation, it will pass and can be replaced by something better. Personal hope calls for action; hope directed towards others calls for support. Always hope is associated with energy directed at an intention and a result. An acronym for hope could be *Human Opportunity Powered by Energy*.

In his book, *Man's Search for Meaning*, Viktor Frankel describes his experiences while being incarcerated in several Nazi concentration camps, including Auschwitz, during World War Two. He noticed that those most likely to survive their ordeal were the people who hoped for a better future and believed they would be liberated. Their hope sustained them and helped them weather successfully the stress, hunger, fear and human misery generated by the circumstances of camp life. Hope is an antidote to depression, because it points to the fact that whatever the circumstance a person finds themselves in, it can always get better.

There are many documented cases of medical "miracles" where people pronounced "hopeless cases" with terminal illnesses and life-threatening conditions would unexpectedly recover and return to good health. "Where there is life, there is hope," the saying goes. The word hopeless should be struck from the dictionary. A person can always engender hope into any situation; it is a matter of being prepared to "look on the bright side" and hope for the best. It is essential not to do so in a vague, undefined sort of way, but with definition and power. The more specific details a person can bring to the situation they hope for, the more power they can add to their image of the future and the more likely their hope will become a reality.

When you say to someone, "I hope you get better soon," in your mind, do you leave the task of recuperation entirely up to them, or do you send them a little bit of your own energy, consciously and deliberately, with which they might regain their strength that much faster and more effectively?

The future is not fixed and as long as it remains in a fluid state (in other words, it is not yet solidified by becoming the present), it can be influenced by our thoughts and our hope. "Hope springs eternal," another saying goes. Hope is like a fishing line, cast to the future. The difference between a successful angler and one who throws the line randomly and wishes for the best is experience and having developed an intuition about the habits of fish. Hope becomes reality when we apply our mind, soul and senses to power our desires and follow them up with action. A person who hopes to catch fish but never goes out with their fishing rod will never have their hopes come true.

Sometimes it is better not to know what is considered impossible, so that our range of perceived possibilities do not become limited. In the 70s there was a group of Rumanian gymnasts who awed the world with their abilities and strength. Nadia Comăneci won five gold medals, three silver and one bronze at the Montreal and Moscow Olympics in 1976 and 1980. She also won a number of gold and silver medals in European and World Championships, and there were others who followed in her footsteps. When interviewed, their coach explained that he had never told the girls what the world records were, so they could not feel limited by the achievements of others.

When people say, "You can't," or "It cannot be done," don't believe them! Find out for yourself. What might be indeed impossible for one person, might be an easy target for someone else. Of all the energetic qualities, hope is the miracle worker. So when people say, "Don't get your hopes up," perhaps ignore them and always have your hopes up and ready to spring into action!

Hope gives us an outlook on the future—we hope things can improve and be better. "Let's hope for the best," we might say. But it might be that we are simply hoping in a passive way, while we await the outcome tomorrow might bring or we wish someone else would bail us out of a difficult situation. When we hope, are we attempting to actively influence the future? If you hope for longevity, for example, do you exercise and eat well?

Longevity is possible. In the book, *What Makes Olga Run?* Bruce Grierson describes a woman in her 90s who competes as an athlete within her age category and has many gold medals to show for it. Hoping for a long, healthy life is a very practical pursuit. Jeanne Calment, who died in 1997, lived 122 years and 164 days. She was the longest living person on record. There are stories of a man who lived in China—Li Ching-Yuen—who supposedly had lived either 197 or 256 years, depending upon which account of his life one reads. It seems that the human body was made to last; as long as we treat it with respect and give it what it needs to flourish, we, too, can hope for long, healthy lives.

False hope can be a denial of our own power, but in the true meaning of the word hope is accompanied by action and intent.

Exercise

Write down what you hope for: for you, for your family, for your country, for the world. (When you hope for someone else, make sure it is something they would hope for for themselves. Otherwise you could be hoping against their own wishes and desires.)

Make this a regular practice.

What do you hope for in one year, two years, five years? If you are clear about what you hope for, it has much more of a chance to become a reality. If you write it down and look at it often, you are giving it definition and powering it with your energy.

Exercise

Every time you use the word hope, imagine a lance of power emitting from the area of your third eye (in the middle of the forehead) into the future. Send the image of what it is you hope for into the future—to a time when you would want your projection to come true.

Meditation

Project five years ahead. Now break it into five steps. What do you hope for for each of the five years?

HOPE

Hope is the optimist who looks ahead with glee
As she thinks of all the things she would like to be.
Then hope imagines better times ahead,
Ignoring the failures, it plans victories instead.
Then it takes up residence with those who are ill
And gives them strength to get better, charging their will.
Then it springs to action with a purpose and a zest
Believing life is for a reason and our function is to quest.
Then hope turns to belief and together they define
Every possible result as better and refined.
Finally hope is everywhere, always and forever there
Ready to assist, to heal and repair.

HOPE (2)

At first hope is the dream of the lost
Searching for land in a landless sea,
Looking at the horizon to see a coast
Heralding that the future is something to be.
Then hope transforms into a beacon of light
Lighting the way for those yet to come,
Guiding the searcher through the darkening night
With a vision of what can be done.
Then hope emerges with a new disguise
Offering optimism and a positive view,
It says all is well and looks with bright eyes
Into the future with a vigor new.
Then hope becomes a feeling that is hard to resist—
It passes from person to person, lifting their mood;
It heals and it eases, ready to assist,
Better than any physical food.
Then hope is active and brings action to play
It's a goal, aim or target that beckons and shines;
It promises tomorrow will be a better day
That someone on Earth there are gentler climes.
Then hope surrenders to a higher plan
Petitioning for help it asks from above;
It brings union and harmony
'tween the universe and man
And is akin to its sister—love.
In its next incarnation, hope becomes us
We are the future who herald the new:
A new human model is here—without fanfare or fuss
It could be me; it could be you.

Humility

Humility is a reminder that we are
not alone and are here as part of
a greater universal plan and purpose.

CHAPTER FIVE

Humility

*H*umility is knowing one's position as a human within the bigger picture of the universe. Understanding the vastness of Creation causes a person to become humble. The other side of humility is understanding the greatness of the human spirit and appreciating the impact we have on the energy fields around us. We are small on the one hand and great on the other. Humility is a seer that looks both ways.

Appreciating our privileged position in God's Creation brings gratitude which is akin to humility. One way to connect to humility is to contemplate the engineering of the human design. Intricate, precise, effective are some words that might come to mind to describe it. Another way to connect to humility is to contemplate the vastness and precision of the universe. Both designs—the human's and Creation's—can only give rise to awe, which brings with it a sense of humility.

When looking up humility in the dictionary, the definition speaks of modesty and weakness, but these are outward portrayals of humility that may or may not stem from true humility. There is a fine line between humility and lack of self-worth. True humility comes from an inner strength and an appreciation of one's position and station. As a human, surrounded by God's Creation and all the marvels of universal laws and their manifestation on Earth, how can a person not be humble? A lack of humility, which can be described as arrogance or superiority, comes from an inflated view of oneself and one's importance. It can also come from a deflated view of oneself, in which case it could be described as a lack of self-worth.

To have humility is to be able to view not only oneself but everything one comes into contact with from a greater perspective. Take the simple, non-personal example of day or night. We say, "It is daytime," but that is our personal view, because on the other side of the planet it is night. We humans live in the eternal alternation between day and night, hot and cold, or good and bad. But the planet has a different experience. Imagine that you are a planet hurtling through space—immediately your view elevates because now in your mind you are experiencing day and night—both—all the time. The planet is always experiencing not only day and night, but also dawn and dusk, so by imagining you are the planet, you now have these four experiences happening simultaneously. The other extremes, like hot and cold, are also present at all times on planet Earth as well as many other manifestations of the law of duality.

We might be at the center of *our* world, but we are not at the center of *the* world. Simply remembering that this is so and that for every extreme we might experience there is always the opposite happening somewhere else and that it is being experienced by someone else, is an aid to finding humility.

Humility might be related to modesty, but it runs deeper and is connected to a person's development and world view. It might produce modesty as an end result, but it is based in a very sober and realistic view of one's abilities and possibilities. It doesn't mean underestimating the power of each human and their potential as they live their life, but it recognizes the greater powers in the universe that can move a person and work through them. It also recognizes that the person does not possess these great universal powers they can connect to, but can become a receptor and transmitter of these high energies.

"It moved me to write this book," a person might say, recognizing the power of the essence that had inspired them, rather than "I wrote this book." This would be a true expression of humility.

Lack of humility can go two ways and cause two different reactions—either, "I am nothing" or, "I am full of self importance."

Think of the exercise of a group of people sitting in a boat in the middle of an ocean when it is decided that one person needs to be thrown overboard for the others to survive. Who is it going to be? One person might be preoccupied by the need to save themselves while another might volunteer to go overboard to save the others. However, the object of the exercise is to dismiss both these views and to find the truth of the situation—who is the weakest link. Who would be the least useful in terms of helping the group survive in the conditions that the people in the boat might come across—lack of food, water and perhaps trying to survive on a desert island? What are the necessary skills to survive? What are the criteria in making such a choice, rather than responding from a personal bias or emotional extreme?

Humility allows a person to admit when they are wrong. If guilty, humility encourages a person to admit to their guilt and to confess. It also allows a person to offer themselves forgiveness and tolerance as they learn—the same treatment they would offer to any other person. In response to any mistake—whether committed by another person or oneself—it is important to condemn the act, not the person. A parent should never say "bad boy," or "naughty girl." It is the act that was wrong or naughty, not the child. Humility offers forgiveness and a second (or third) chance. Humiliation transfers the guilt to the person; humility pins the guilt to the action.

When in depression and sadness, humility brings with it the understanding that in that state a person's view is distorted and so it allows them to remember they are not as bad as they think they are. This realization can lift a person up. When in success and victory, a person should remember they are not as good as they think they are and humility will consequently bring them down to size. In ancient Rome, following a victory, when a general or statesman was given a triumph, as they paraded through the streets in a chariot, their slave would be standing behind them, whispering in their ear, "Remember you are mortal," or the Latin words, "*Memento mori*" (remember death).

Humility is a realization that no one is alone; every human is part of a tribe. There are over seven billion people on Earth, so each one of us, no matter how powerful, rich, famous and talented, is only one seven billionth part of the river of humanity. Every day people are born and people die. With humility it becomes clear that life is short and no matter how influential we might be into our community, and how effective our works, they will be gone with time, as well as the memory of our journey through life.

According to the Chinese philosopher Lao-Tzu and author of the *Tao Te Ching*, true humility can be seen when it is accompanied by service. An illumined person understands that in order to connect to higher energies one must reach out to others and offer one's time and resources to help those in need. Being humble is to make no false claims and to give without counting the cost.

A person who lacks humility has an unrealistic view of themselves. They think they are either greater than they are or smaller than they are. A person who thinks they are greater than they are might be referred to as being "too big for their boots" or "britches." They could also be referred to as committing the sin of pride (one of the seven deadly vices). When a person realizes that they are not as capable as they had thought they were—perhaps they had attempted to do something and had fallen short of their target—it is often said that they had tasted "humble pie."

Humility calls for true assessment. Lack of humility takes a person into fantasy, above all about themselves.

The Chinese word for humility consists of two characters, meaning confident, yet empty. True humility gives a person confidence, because they know who they are and how they fit into the scheme of things. The emptiness is their ability to learn and to connect to other people. A humble person is able to listen to another and to share their joys and their grief. An energy healer needs a dose of humility because it is never the healer who heals, but the energy they are connecting to and channeling to help their patient. A real healer makes no claims but sees themselves as an instrument of Creation. The moment a healer thinks it is their energy that is doing the healing, the healing channel becomes blocked and the healing energy can no longer flow through the healer into their patient.

To become a self-healer a person needs humility. With every injury or disease, there are two healings that can take place, not one. The first is the cure of the illness itself, but the second—which requires humility—is to forgive oneself for contracting the disease or for injuring oneself. If, for example, a person falls down the stairs, it is because they were not paying attention and had lost their focus. Humility will allow them to acknowledge their clumsiness, to forgive themselves and move on. A person with humility will never fall down the stairs twice because after the first time they will realize that stairs can be dangerous and one needs to pay attention to where they place their feet, whether climbing or descending. This statement is based on the author's personal experience. Having fallen down a flight of stairs and broken my shoulder, I now am very careful every time I climb or walk down stairs. Following my fall I realized I needed to forgive myself for causing the injury, before I could fully heal and recover.

Humility allows a person to recognize the achievements of others and to give credit where credit is due. A humble person's "opponents" are considered to be worthy, otherwise their wins would be a small merit indeed. It is important to praise others and to never underestimate another person's struggle. However, it is also important that such praise should be genuine and heartfelt.

Humility recognizes not only the achievements, but also the struggles of others. It causes a person to be tolerant and realize that other people believe in other gods and live in different realities. With humility life becomes so much more interesting, because we learn to listen to other people and to appreciate the environment. Humility therefore brings learning and the joy of discovery in its wake.

If care defines your relationship with and attitude to others, hope is a lance and a vision into the future, then humility is all about a person's self-view. We need to think of ourselves within the context of other people. Most probably we are not the best at whatever it is we do and most probably not the worst. But one thing is certain: we are the only one of us—totally unique. Humility is honoring that uniqueness and being open to who we might become.

Most people become limited at some point in their life by the opinions of others, by their education and by their view of themselves. Humility supports the understanding that we do not know the full picture of who we are and why we are here on planet Earth at this time. Humility causes a person to ask questions, such as, "Who am I?" and "How can I fulfill my potential?" A person might be employed as a doctor, a teacher or a secretary, but humility will tell them that that is not who they are. If we do not identify with a specific job, even if we consider it to be a good job, we will be far more open to becoming the best we can be, which is not limited to a single profession.

Humility brings a person into the view that as long as they live, they are an integral part of the planetary ecology. Just as we are alive, so is the planet, only her lifespan is much greater than ours. We are living inside the ecology of Geo and are energetically (as well physically) contributors to her atmosphere. Humility brings with it appreciation and gratitude for the life we were given and tells us to pay back by looking after the planetary ecology, rather than destroying it.

We humans are spiritual beings and we inhabit a vast universe. Our sojourn on planet Earth is brief and we do not know what our next destination, after this life, might be. Something wanted us to be here and great efforts have been made to bring us to this point—to be born, to be fed, clothed, schooled and loved; to be energetically and physically nourished and sustained. It would take a great warehouse to store all the food any one adult person has eaten in their lifetime and which the planet has provided for us throughout our lives (not to mention the water and air we have also consumed). It is a humbling thought to think about all the gifts we have received to make our lives begin and continue.

Humility is not taking anything for granted. The world or other people do not owe us a living. Therefore any act of kindness should be greeted with appreciation and value. These are the keyways towards humanity.

Another keyway to humility is remembering that we are mortal. We are here on Earth for a very short time and it is always good to keep that perspective in mind, so that humility can become our companion. Whatever we accomplish in this life has a limited lifespan. Even though we might leave behind us works of art or writings, monuments or even buildings or masterpieces—they will all eventually become forgotten and will inevitably turn to dust. Humility allows us to be realistic about our abilities and future without taking away from our hope and appreciation of the true genius that each human represents.

Exercise
Walk into your bedroom as if it belonged to someone you had never met (like policemen on *Law and Order* going into a deceased person's apartment, looking for clues). Write down five things you notice about this person.

Exercise
What are your five best qualities? What are your five worst qualities?

Examples:
messy—tidy
loyal—disloyal
punctual—tardy
demonstrative—taciturn
focused—distracted
careful—careless
tolerant—demanding
happy—sad
disappointed—glad

Find nuances to describe the exact qualities you represent.

Meditation

Picture your place in the scheme of things:

1. Picture yourself as one speck in the universe.

2. Picture yourself in your close-in domain (your home, your work, your family, your friends).

HUMILITY

At first humility says I am not alone
And the heart is not there to resemble a stone.
Then it recognizes there are others like me
And causes me to be grateful for all that I see.
All that I hear now brings joy to my souls—
The sound of the waves and the bell as it tolls.
Nature is humble as it fulfills its part,
So I try to be my best and make a good start,
Knowing that always there is room to improve
As I value my body and the fact I can move.
So many gifts I received in my days
So humility gives me the strength to remember to praise
All that is natural, the universe and man
And the fact there is a greater, long term, working plan.

HUMILITY (2)

In humility I give thanks
I could never do it alone—
It takes two to tango and a team to dance
It took two willing parents for me to be born.
I am what I am, not the best and not the worst
Struggling to be better every day;
There is no law that says I should be first;
It's enough that I can forge my way.
Nature supports me and so do my friends,
I am rich beyond measure and glad;
Whatever the universe delivers and sends
I should learn and never label it bad.

A LEAF

A dried-up leaf, crumpled and old
What are the stories you have never told?
Settled to your lot to be discarded and shed
Making way for new growth to take your place instead.
Back in the springtime you were only a bud
Now trampled and brown, underfoot in the mud
I take from you your humility and the decree
That every spring there will always be
new leaves on the tree.

Patience

*Patience reminds us that everything
has its seasons and its timings.*

CHAPTER SIX

Patience

When asked about patience, most people will say it is the ability to wait without getting flustered. Patients in hospitals, whether they are there for an operation or convalescence, know they need to give the healing process its time. After a procedure a doctor might say, "You will not be able to use your hand (run, exercise...) for six weeks," and we accept his verdict with stoicism and patience, mentally projecting ourselves beyond the healing period.

Herbalists and Ayurveda medicine practitioners know that the treatment needs to continue even after the symptoms have disappeared. Often people assume that because the symptoms have ceased, they are cured, but this is often not the case; sometimes if a patient discontinues taking the prescribed herbal or homeopathic remedies too soon, the symptoms will recur.

The ability to wait successfully depends on the person's knowledge and their understanding that everything takes time. Just as one has to wait to the fall to pick the apples growing in an orchard, so does everything have its season. A baby cannot learn to run before it has leaned to walk; a girl cannot become pregnant before she goes through puberty.

Young children mostly do not understand the concept of "tomorrow" or when an adult says, "Wait until you are older to understand." They live in the present and do not worry about the future. A four-year-old son of the author's friend threw his handful of coins out the car window because he was told that the toy shop was closed, but would re-open the next day. For him, "tomorrow" simply did not exist.

Any process takes time. Change takes time. Growing up takes time. Patience is a useful quality to have when one is attempting to implement change. Have you noticed how some days everything seems difficult and nothing goes right, whereas on another day, the most difficult tasks are completed with ease? Sometimes it is best to wait until the energy of the day is conducive to sorting through the jobs that need to be done; because sometimes trying to get through the day feels like a struggle with no results to show for it. In olden days people used to consult an astrologer to find the most auspicious time for a ceremony, to set out on a trip or to initiate a business venture. Sometimes it is possible to "go with the flow" and let the energy current of the day carry you. Going "against the flow" can be very costly both in terms of energy and time expenditure. However, sometimes it is not possible to wait for the right time because a job or task needs to be completed on time. Other times going with the nature of the day allows a person to find connections to original and unusual energies which other people are perhaps not connecting to. The wisdom is to know when to go with the flow and when to go against the flow.

Here on planet Earth construction takes time. Introducing a new endeavor or business requires patience. However, destruction can happen in the blink of an eye. Destruction does not require patience, but to rebuild and start again does. Perhaps elsewhere there are planets where construction is fast but destruction is slow. But we are here on planet Earth where we are subject to her laws, her seasons and her timings.

Learning patience involves reading the energetic trends of the day or detecting the energy within a relationship as it evolves and changes with each encounter and exchange. For example, the Monday blues is a very real energy state: it is caused by millions of people having to go to a job they do not enjoy after having had a weekend spent with their family and friends, doing what they love to do (whatever that is). It is also the day that is influenced by the moon (according to the Babylonians). The moon gives it its name—Monday is moon day. The moon has a strong pull on the magnetic field of the planet and on the human energy field as well. This is why there are more cases of hemorrhaging during a full moon and why more girls and women menstruate during that time of month.

One can be patient (or impatient) with another person who is slow to learn or with a child who "doesn't know better"—this kind of patience is akin to tolerance or understanding. Some people seem to have a natural wealth of this kind of patience. These are the best teachers and young lives benefit from their ability to go over an exercise or tasking again and again until all the pupils get it and understand what is expected of them.

Patience is always associated with timing and waiting for the right time. But what if time is not linear? Can we connect to things "out of season"? Can we conjure up the essence of, say, an apple, before it has a chance to ripen and grow? Can we connect to knowledge without learning? Stories abound about people who are unexpectedly able to perform tasks and demonstrate skills they were not aware they had, and perform them well. A friend of the author was training to be a pilot, when unexpectedly he astonished both himself and his instructor by performing acrobatic maneuvers in the air, flying upside down and landing flawlessly. He was not able to repeat this extraordinary performance until he was fully trained and had been qualified as a licensed pilot. His explanation is that he was open that day to the energies he encountered in the cockpit of the plane and had somehow connected to the trace and history of another pilot (or pilots) who had previously flown the plane and had left behind an energetic trace of their knowledge and skill.

The author had the experience of going into a new high-level secretarial job requiring her to use a dictation machine. The evening before the job was due to start I imagined using such a machine, though I had never seen one in my life prior to this. The next day I sat down at my desk, turned the machine on and knew exactly how to operate it without being shown how. I too felt I had connected to the energies of previous secretaries who had sat in the same chair before me.

In December 2001 in the British Medical Journal, Leonard Leibovici published an article in which he presented the results of a study he had conducted at the Rabin Medical Center in Petah Tiqva in Israel. A group of 3,393 adult patients diagnosed with blood infection between 1919 and 1996 were randomly divided into two groups: a control group and an intervention group. A remote, retroactive intercessory prayer was said for the well-being and full recovery of the intervention group, but not the control group. When consequently the medical records of these patients were checked, it came to light that the mortality rate in the intervention group had been lesser and that their stay in hospital was four times shorter than among the members of the control group.

These results have brought about a further discussion and further tests, conducted by eminent representatives of the medical and scientific worlds, in which they have been further investigating the power and validity of prayer on the one hand and the relativity of our linear concept of time on the other.

Whatever the explanation, there are stories of people connecting to energies from the past and from the future; there are also stories of people "following their instinct" and, for example, performing life-saving surgeries in wartime without any anatomy training or previous experience.

The history of everything that has ever happened in the world is contained within the "astral light" and sometimes the veil between the energy worlds and the material worlds becomes thin and a person can connect to events that had happened in the past, especially if they were emotionally charged, like the history of a battlefield or a murder. This would explain why some houses appear to be haunted and why sometimes people can see and/or hear ghosts.

One can also connect to the energy of a place from a distance. This is one of the reasons why meditation is such a powerful tool. If one can imagine a special place, or picture a place where one had been and found beautiful and healing, that energy is still there and can be connected to through meditation (and with practice). All energies that had ever been created still exist and can be connected to and brought into one's energy field.

The author spent six months isolated in a foreign country when she contracted TB at the age of seven. Missing my family and my home, I decided that if I just quietly lay on my bed, closed my eyes and pretended I was home, maybe it could feel like home. After all, lying on a bed is still lying on a bed, wherever it takes place. I did so and was quite amazed at the result: I felt calmer and much more settled. Since then I have believed in the power of the imagination to reach out and connect to energies, feelings and sensations at distance.

One way to understand a quality is to look at what it is not, or to look at its opposite. Impatience (the opposite of patience) is the inability to tolerate idleness or excessive waiting times. Impatience creates an energetic space within which patience cannot abide. Patience is everything impatience is not. Patience has a sense of serenity about it; impatience is connected to a nervy, disjointed energy. It is the kind of energy that is anti-thesis to the energy needed for meditation, relaxation and healing.

Is impatience always bad? Or should we be impatient with those who are, say, cruel to an animal?

When urgency is called for, like in an emergency, patience is still the best companion to have at one's side. When training for any emergency situation, like CPR, it is still necessary to be cool, collected and assess the situation first.When there was a gas leak in the author's kitchen, the man who arrived at the house, sent by the gas board, was slow, deliberate and very precise with his actions and movements. He did not spend time listening to our evaluation of the situation but went straight to the stove to assess where the leak was coming from for himself. Military special units are trained that urgent speed is slow; very slow and deliberate.

How do the unseen worlds feel about us? Are they sometimes impatient with us because we don't get the point or we do things that are harmful or detrimental to our chosen purpose or to the environment? What about the human race? How does the planet feel? Is she impatient with us and our heaps of garbage? How much longer will she suffer our cruelty, pollution, greed?

When is a good time to worship? Is it a Sunday, when the Christians go to church, a Saturday when the Jews go to the synagogue or a Friday when the Muslims go to the mosque? Or perhaps there is no bad timing for prayer and worship or meditation or contemplation; perhaps they can indeed happen any day of the week and any time of day.

The laws of nature affect the material worlds differently than the material worlds. For example, in the material worlds hot air rises, whereas in the energy worlds hot energy sinks to the ground. There are two aspects to timing and two ways one can connect to the energy of patience. In the material worlds, time is linear, or at least this is how we perceive it. In the energy worlds time does not exist. Energetically there is a me and a you of all ages and all possibilities into the future.

The moment a person makes a choice and acts upon it, they bring something from the energy worlds into the material arena. An idea or an inspiration is an energy coming into one's energy field. Acting on it is bringing that energy into one's aura and transforming it into energy that with patience can become an inspiration to others. Being patient with oneself is giving oneself time to discover what is the unique gifting one can offer into the world. So in the material worlds one needs patience to see results from one's endeavors. But in the energy worlds results can occur instantaneously, surprising us with immediate transformation or change.

Patience in the material worlds is the ability to wait for the right time or the right season to complete a task or for a process to come to fruition.

Patience in the energy worlds is the ability to connect to the relevant energy, regardless of timing, to complete a task or bring a process to fruition.

PATIENCE

At first patience is the ability to wait
And not expect results straight out of the gate.
Then it is knowledge that everything takes time—
It only takes a moment to commit a crime
To destroy or to hurt, to maim or to kill,
But years to grow up or to learn a new skill.
Patience is harmony with Creation's ways;
There are cycles and seasons that affect us all.
The universe knows not tardiness or delays
And works perfectly to natural law.

Gratitude

*Gratitude connects us to the source of our health
and well being; it brings us closer to
higher universal energies.*

Gratitude

Gratitude is akin to respect because it too makes a person appreciate what they are and who they are. Gratitude reaches out to the universe or to God or to destiny—because gratitude is usually directed at someone or something, whether defined and identified or not. Who, or what are we grateful to? The answer to this question might differ from person to person. Who, for example, are we grateful to for the gift of life? Yes, we were born of our parents, but who or what decided we should be the unique person that we are? Did we petition to be born? If so, why now and why here? Of course, we cannot answer these questions in a definitive way, but contemplating them can indeed deepen the quality and extent of our gratitude.

The state of being grateful allows a person to appreciate the many gifts they have received. The fact of being born is the first gift and with it came a whole package of working parts—eyes, organs, senses, soul, arms, legs—everything in working order. Then came the ability to walk, speak and think—those human attributes that make us unique and special in this world. All these gifts were freely given—we acquired them with little or no effort on our part. And yet, how we use them is a reflection of our gratitude. Do we pay back for existence by how we use our gifts? Do we process fine energies which enhance our surroundings and the planet herself? Do we try to improve, be the best we can be and develop our unique skills and abilities, so we can honestly say we have lived life to the full?

A Garden of Qualities

To live life fully is true gratitude. Each person is unique and has the opportunity to develop that uniqueness into a symphony of expression that no one else can manifest.

There are two kinds of gratitude—directed and general. Directed gratitude is when we are grateful to somebody or something (like an institution) for an identifiable gifting. It can be an event, a relationship, a job or an object. Being grateful is to say thank you and show our appreciation. Perhaps we reciprocate another's kindness with a gift or a letter. Then we feel the matter is closed—a gift begets a gift or a fitting response. But the general gratitude never ends. It has no beginning and no end, because it is a natural feeling that accompanies the gift of life. It is not directed to any specific person or deity, but it is an energy that we send into the universe as we thank the powers that have given us life and continue to support us every single day.

Gratitude is a heartfelt thank you that lives in a person's energy field and radiates out from their aura into their surroundings. It becomes activated when a person consciously adds up that they are glad to be alive. Personal gratitude is then added to the essence of gratitude that lives in the world and it will cause others who know and value us to be grateful for our existence as well. Thus gratitude can grow and by contagion cause others to be stopped in their tracks to appreciate the small things in life, like the beauty of a flower or the song of a bird, as well as the big things, like the relationship with one's spouse or one's parents or one's children. There is so much to be grateful for—just look around you and open your eyes to the beauty of nature and the intricacies of your own engineering.

There is a scene in the television series, *John Adams* when in his old age the former president stops while walking in a field with a friend and drops down on his knees to express adoration to the Creator for making a thing of beauty as simple and perfect as a small field flower. This attitude of gratitude is often a gifting that comes to a person later in life (as in the example of John Adams), when one can appreciate and value the seemingly small things in life, which hold a great power of connection to the forces of the universe.

Being grateful connects a person to great things. For example, if we are grateful for our relationship with our partner, we will address our gratitude to whatever it was that had brought us together in the first place. You can call it kismet or fate, or even go as far as adding up that there are frequencies in this world that are attracted to each other and that the Law of Attraction was active in that circumstance of your first meeting.

Belief in the Law of Attraction brings this energetic law into one's awareness and can be instrumental in activating it (setting it in motion) in order to achieve one's desires in the future. Gratitude is a great place to start. It acknowledges that there are forces and energies that are greater than ourselves and are at play all the time, working for us (on our behalf) even while we sleep.

Gratitude can connect us to great energies and can cause them to take notice of our endeavors. Just as we like to be appreciated and acknowledged if we give someone a present or help them out in some way, so do universal energies. Being grateful is like sending a thank you note to the universe. Having received our thanks, Creation is so much more likely to help us on our way again. It is like building a highway along which good energies and progressive circumstances can come our way and enhance our future.

A Garden of Qualities

Gratitude for the Planet Meditation
Earth

Imagine walking barefoot in the sand on a warm beach. Try to imagine the feeling of being connected to the earth. Think how the earth is always beneath our feet, even under concrete or several feet below, if we are on a higher floor of a building.

Think of planting a seed in the ground and over time watching a seedling appear above ground, reaching toward the sun.

The earth is a propagator of all floral life—it does not discriminate, but gives nourishment to all organic life which in turn brings sustenance to our daily lives—providing us with food, fuel and many things we eat, own and process. The earth also supports fauna life which provides us with food, service, clothing and companionship. Always there, the earth supports our every step.

Mentally express gratitude to the earth. Take a moment to do this.

Water

Think of a warm shower after a sweaty workout or after a particularly dirty, grimy job, like digging in the garden, repairing a car or cleaning an oven. Think how refreshing, invigorating and cleansing that feels. Take a moment to do this.

Now think of a swim in the sea on a hot summer's day. The sun is beating down, but the cool, cleansing waters keep you feeling refreshed and cleansed. Take a moment to do this.

Now think of a mountain stream high up in the mountains—the pure waters are fresh enough to drink. They taste so clean and refreshing after an arduous climb to these high elevations.

Now mentally express your gratitude to the water, which is always there for you, on tap, ready to quench your thirst, cleanse your body and invigorate all your inner lives. Take a moment to do this.

Air

Think of a walk in a forest on a warm day. Breathe in deeply and feel the fresh air filling your lungs. Take another deep breath and imagine the energized oxygen traveling throughout your body within your blood. Take a moment to do this.

Now look up at the sky which is clear blue in color. You are looking at a whole expanse of air all around you and above your head. This protective layer of air supports your life and separates you from harmful radiation. Take a moment to picture this.

The air supports your every breath, every moment of your life without any conscious effort on your part. It is always there for you, free and willing to oblige, Take a moment to express your gratitude for the air.

Fire

Think of a warm fire on a cold winter's evening. Imagine you are stretching your hands toward the burning logs and imagine the heat spreading throughout your whole body. Take a moment to feel this.

Imagine the glow of a candle illuminating the darkness of a room; imagine your ancestors sitting together around a table, and how the family circle is lit up by candlelight. Take a moment to picture this.

Imagine a camp fire somewhere out in the wilderness and a group of friends sitting around the fire, telling stories and sharing their experiences of the day. Now mentally express your gratitude for the fire, which gives warmth and sustains life. Take a moment to do this.

Energy

Imagine that you can see energy. Imagine walking down a busy street and all you see are not physical people but colorful, pulsating, illuminated egg-shaped auras walking alongside you and opposite you. The entire street is pulsating with energy—everything processes energy; every atom, every tree, every car is emanating energy—all different colors and hues. Take a moment to picture this.

Now imagine you are taking a walk in the country. The energies emanating from the trees, the flowers, the grass and the animals are so clean and bright. Energy is everywhere. Take a moment to imagine this.

Now imagine that in that setting you are looking at your hand. You notice the illumination coming out of the trips of your fingers. White is emanating from your thumb, red from the pointing finger, blue from the middle finger, yellow from the ring finger and green from the little finger, also known as the "pinky." Take a moment to imagine this.

Now imagine yourself sleeping in your bed. Imagine a shaft of energy entering your body and your soul—energy which allows you to act, be, feel and do. It is the life-giving force supplied by the planet that supports your life every minute of every day. Take a moment to picture this.

Now take a moment to mentally express your gratitude for the energy that supports and enhances your life.

Gratitude For Others Meditation

Think of five people that are closest to you—family, friends or colleagues. It can include someone who has passed on or someone who is currently at physical distance from you. Take a moment to do this.

Take the first person who is closest to you. Think of an incident between you that has caused you to feel love for this person, or appreciation or inspiration or joy or all of the above. Take a moment to do this.

Now mentally express gratitude to this person for this special moment and all the special moments you have shared. Take a moment to do this.

Now repeat this process for the other four people you have thought of.

Gratitude For Self Meditation

1. What are the odds of your mother meeting your father?
There are over seven billion people in the world, so each man has approximately a one in three billion chance of meeting any particular woman at any particular time.

Take a moment to contemplate these odds.

2. What is the chance of your mother and father conceiving you on a particular day?
If the relationship was a lasting one and if your mother's childbearing years lasted for, say, 20 years, there would have been approximately a one in 7,300 chance that you would have been conceived on any one particular day within that timeframe.

Take a moment to contemplate these odds.

3. What is the chance of you being who you are, decided by your unique DNA and gender?
On that very day that your parents came together to

conceive you, your father would have produced millions of sperm, each one of which would have carried a slightly different DNA sequence. It was your father's sperm that determined your gender.

Take a moment to contemplate these odds.

4. What is the chance of your mother's ovum carrying the particular genes that have contributed to making you exactly who you are?

During her childbearing years a woman's ovaries release on average one egg every 28 days. Assuming she would not conceive between 15 and 18 or between 45 and 50, that leaves 27 years with 13 lunar months each—351 in all. If a child were conceived during any other month, it would have had a different DNA sequence.

If you have a sibling—their DNA will be similar to yours, yet different, conceived of a different sperm and ovum. Only you, conceived at the exact time you were conceived, have your physiognomy, traits and abilities in your exact combination. Even identical twins with the same DNA develop different characters as their genetics alter and change throughout life.

Take a moment to contemplate these odds.

5. What is the chance that on that day your father's sperm impregnated your mother's ovum?

This is an unknown, but pregnancy is actually a comparatively rare occurrence, as compared to the number of intercourses occurring every day. Even if an average family has two or three children, how does that compare to the number of times a couple has sex?

Take a moment to contemplate these odds.

6. What is the chance of an impregnated egg being carried to full term?

It is estimated that half of the number of conceived eggs are lost during the first week of pregnancy, with the woman often not even knowing that she had been pregnant. Then there are the added obstacles of complications during pregnancy, miscarriages and abortions.

Take a moment to contemplate these odds.

7. What are the chances of a child being born healthy and capable of growing up to become an adult, able to read this book?
Childbirth and childhood mortality are higher in some countries than in other places where prenatal and child care are more advanced, so it would depend upon where you were born.

Take a moment to contemplate these odds.

Having added up all these odds that have come together to make it possible for each unique human to be born onto Earth, how can a person not be confident that they are meant to be here, that there is a reason and purpose for their existence and that Creation wants and needs them to be here—with their unique fingerprints, DNA and characteristics?

Take a moment to mentally express your gratitude for your life.

Generosity

Giving to others is paying back for the universal gifting
we have enjoyed by being born and
receiving our many skills and abilities.

CHAPTER EIGHT

Generosity

*G*enerosity is the ability or the preponderance to give. There are many ways in which a person can demonstrate generosity, but the most valuable commodity they have to give at their disposal is their time. We have a limited supply of time and the older we get, the clearer it becomes that time is becoming ever more precious. A young person often squanders their time and this is natural because they are in the age of experimentation and finding out who they are, what they can do and what their life is all about. When a person makes a decision as to their life's journey and when they embark upon a mission and a goal, time becomes more valuable because now it is purposeful and can be put to good use. So who and what you then give your time to becomes a question of discernment because the gift of time, once given, is not going to be able to ever be taken back or given again. With age one learns to not only value one's own time but also the time shared with others. An older person learns to appreciate the generosity offered by others who decide to spend time with them.

Generosity can be expressed in many ways. We can give our money to charity or bestow gifts upon others. In medieval times there was the custom of giving away a tithe, which is a tenth of one's income, to charity or to the church. It is a good practice to give to those who are less fortunate than ourselves to thereby help release suffering in this world. Most people in the West are among the wealthier 10% of the world's population. Our tithes, which is not much to us, can help many. It is our duty to play our part and reach out to those who need our help and support.

Generosity is more than giving away money, goods or time. It is an attitude and a soul preponderance. It is a knowing that during our lifetime we are not alone and that others need us, just as we need them. This knowing will bring about a generosity of the spirit. We receive energy from the planet, from nature and from other people every day. By the same token, we radiate and give away our energy every moment we are alive, whether we are aware of it or not. We radiate into the world our thoughts, feelings and qualities. Every positive action that is connected to the higher realms of the energy worlds helps lift the vibration of our surroundings. Every moment of every day we have a choice whether to be generous or not, happy or not, joyful or not. Becoming a generous person is to deliberately set about to consciously give away our gifts—our wisdom, our skills, our unique abilities and talents. Our generosity of spirit translates into encouragement, healing and the ability to bring out the best in other people.

There is a saying that what goes around, comes around. When one gives of oneself on a repetitive and even habitual basis, one will also receive. People have the need and desire to reciprocate. It might not be the same people who give to us in return, but generosity does have the magical way of repaying in kind.

At the time of a birthday, we say, "Many happy returns," indicating that we wish the person to have many more birthdays. At the same time we are confirming that the wishes, the sentiment as well as even the material presents we give will come back to us. Not necessarily in the same form they are given but perhaps in gratitude and in feelings that are energetic in nature, but are as real and as influential in our life as material objects. In fact, energetic gifts are more permanent because material objects can be lost, destroyed and damaged, but energy cannot be destroyed. It will remain part of one's energy field as long as it is maintained and added to.

So, like all other energetic qualities, generosity needs to be fed on a regular basis to become part of one's radiation and character formation. If you want to be a generous person, give something away often. It does not have to be much—a kind word counts, a note of thanks helps or a coin left on the wall for someone else to find will do the trick. It has to be done consciously, with intent, and the quality of generosity will come to live with you for good. When that happens, you will never want for anything in your life because generosity begets generosity, just as like goes to like.

GENEROSITY

At first generosity is the ability to give,
To help another in their struggle to live.
It partners with charity and asks for a tithe,
So we give away ten percent of what we earn or five.
Then generosity is giving one's time—
It is our most precious gift as it is in decline;
The older we get, the shorter it grows,
Time is our treasure as an old person knows.
Generosity is a cycle, as it turns and comes back
Bringing with it abundance, it abolishes lack.
So lack, which many would see as a flaw
With generosity turns to luck which is a natural law:
You attract what you radiate, if you are true to your core
You will get what you need and won't be asking for more.

Constancy

*Constancy tells us that many small efforts
in one direction is often the keyway to success.*

CHAPTER NINE

Constancy

Constancy is habit forming—through repetition we build our habits until they become part of our make-up and character. Habits are formed in four stages:

1. When you decide to learn or to do something new, like learning to play the piano, learning a new language, inhaling your first cigarette or beginning to play a game, like cards, Scrabble or football, you know the piano exists, you have seen a football game on television, you have been around smokers, but you don't really know yet what is involved. This is the known unknown.

2. Then you start your lessons and you get an idea what is involved. You touch the piano keys and you are shown some simple scales. At first you have a little bit of experience—you can put your first sentences together in a foreign language, but you have to think about it and it all seems so difficult as you struggle to remember the vocabulary. Many people who sign up to learn a new skill, like to speak a foreign language or how to play an instrument, give up at this stage.

3. Then you can begin to speak, you can play melodies, you can read notes. You understand the rules of the game. When you smoke, you no longer cough, you know what to do and how to do it. But you still have to think about what you are doing; it is not yet "second nature" to you. When speaking a foreign language your sentences are haltingly slow and awkward, because you have to think about every word and phrase. However, you can now express yourself so that you are understood.

4. Finally, the activity you have learned is part of your energetic make-up and you no longer have to think about what you are doing. You can play the piano without looking at your hands; when playing football, your legs seem to know where to take you without a conscious thought. Smoking is now a habit which is difficult to break; you reach for a cigarette without thinking. This is the stage when a person becomes really skilled and the new habit no longer involves our conscious thinking, but is a throughout process, involving all parts. This is the known known.

Constancy allows a person to make the journey from the known unknown to the known known. Accompanied by persistence, constancy supports a person in their learning process.

Constancy is a trait that allows another person to be secure that you will not suddenly change or become dangerous or unpredictable in any way. It is offering another person the stability of knowing that you are reliable. However, it does not mean that you will not change; it is simply a guarantee of standards upheld and of courtesy and respect maintained. If it signified no change, constancy would become stagnation. After all, the one constant in our lives is change!

Constancy is a benchmark, an energy frequency you radiate and become known for. When you meet new people, they look for qualities, attitudes and behaviors they can rely on in their association with you.

Constancy is a quality that allows a person to grow other qualities. If a person wishes to become patient, for example, and they add constancy to their efforts, they will indeed become patient. So constancy can help build good habits. The bad habits are never associated with constancy. You do not say, "He is constant in his gambling." More likely you would say that a person is possessed by their bad habits. So constancy is associated with conscious choice, rather than giving up one's right to choose. It is self-induced and self-determined. If you want to be known as a patient, trustworthy, hard-working or honest person, simply add constancy to any of the above-mentioned adjectives, and you will become constant in your efforts to invite your chosen qualities into your life so you can become the person you are striving to be.

Constancy is a universal quality because the universe is constant. So whenever constancy fails us, we can follow the example of the Northern Star and become re-inspired to become constant in our endeavors.

Wisdom

*Wisdom distilled from experience helps a person to
be a good judge of character and to
predict the results of actions taken.*

CHAPTER TEN

Wisdom

*W*isdom comes with age and experience. Simply by living alive we acquire wisdom, because we witness the fact that actions bring consequences, just as we witness the fact that non-action also brings consequences. We learn from experience. When we make a mistake, we learn how to avoid making the same mistake again.

However, some people are wiser than others, even if they have lived the same number of years on planet Earth. Wisdom is not only dependent on a person's longevity, but also on their attitude and willingness to learn. Sometimes we might say about a young person that they are "wise beyond their years." Or we might say about an older person that the fact that they have lived so long is only proof that they have eaten more potatoes than most. (This was one of the favorite sayings of the grandmother of one of the author's friends.)

As well as learning from our own experiences, we can also learn from the experiences of others. That is what parents, teachers, mentors and gurus can provide us with: they share with us their knowledge, their experiences and the wisdom they have distilled from their experiences so we can learn from their knowledge and their mistakes. The acquired wisdom of thousands of writers has given rise to a whole genre of self-help books, which seems to be aggregating daily.

A wise person is a person who has thought deeply about their life—they have distilled from their experiences the wisdom to not only know what actions are beneficial to them and which behaviors to avoid, but they will have also condensed that knowledge into a universal truth that can help any person who might care to ask them for advice.

Wise sayings and folk wisdoms which have been passed down to us through generations come from wise people who through their experience had learned about the best way for a person to be successful and effective in their life. There are many wise folk sayings and folktales in many different languages; there are also many wise instructions by many wise saviors and teachers written down throughout the ages. Whether anonymous or whether the author is known, these oral traditions as well as the world's written heritage are a cornucopia of wisdom, from which we can draw our own best instructions for today's usage.

You will never be able to read and appreciate all the great literature that exists in the world and all the sacred books, hallowed by followers of different religions and traditions. But we can remain open to the wisdoms we do come across in our life and learn from people who have wisdom they are open to share. To become wise, one must be open to learn from the wisdom of others and not be closed or bigoted about another person's beliefs.

There are gems to be found everywhere. A wise person keeps their eyes and ears open because they know that they can learn in the most unexpected circumstances. Everyone has some wisdom to offer. A wise person will view another as a source of wisdom and, given the right circumstance, they will attempt to draw out the best from every person they meet.

In the *Serenity Prayer* it mentions knowing the difference between the things we can change and the things we cannot. For many people comfortability causes them to accept things that they could in fact change, if they had put their mind to it. The wisdom to know what one could

134

change is still no guarantee that one would act to cause a change for the better in one's life. Perhaps one could add another line to that famous prayer: "And give me the courage to act upon that wisdom."

Change can be difficult because we are creatures of habit. But change is a worthwhile pursuit because it brings with it a fresh start and a new beginning. It is an opportunity to reinvent oneself in new circumstances. A wise person embraces change and provokes it in one's life. If we refuse to accept change when the opportunity presents itself, we will never know that perhaps life could have been much better if only we had implemented the change that was on offer.

Sometimes it is worthwhile to initiate change for change's sake because within a new situation one will inevitably learn about oneself and what not to do (as well as what one should be doing).

When going through change—whether it is a new relationship, a new job, moving to a new country or town, or whether it is simply remodeling one's home or taking up a new hobby—one is giving oneself a fresh start. We then can see ourselves in a new light and face new challenges that otherwise we might never know we were capable of taking on.

Wisdom is the continuing attempt to be the best one can be—always finding new challenges and new experiences. Wisdom is learning from each new experience and embodying that learning so that it lives within one's energy field. When a person is truly wise, other people will recognize their wisdom; the evidence and confirmation of one's wisdom lies in the fact that others will seek one's advice.

So who are the wise people? Those who have the best advice to give and those who follow their own best counsel.

A Garden of Qualities

Do you consider yourself to be wise? If you do, listen to your own advice. Sometimes it is easier to see what others should be doing in their lives, rather than implementing the same advice into one's own life. Wisdom allows a person become their own mentor and teacher.

WISDOM
I question whether wisdom comes with age
But if it does, when will I become a sage?
What do I have to do to be wise?
Will it grow on me gradually or come as a surprise?

One thing about being wise I think is nice—
You can tell others what to do and give them advice.
You can say what you think and act without a pretext
You will be able to predict the future,
and anticipate what is next.

Courage

*Courage releases us from
the shackles of fear and brings with it
new opportunity and the ability to do.*

CHAPTER ELEVEN

Courage

Courage is the ability to break one's own stop situation and enter into new domains. It is the ability to overcome fear and/or pain and to move into the next stage of one's development, whatever that might be. It is being able to come out of *our cage* (which is an anagram of *courage*) and being prepared to foster the future and what IT needs. Courage is being able to view life not as a personal challenge, but having the ability to have the insight to surrender to a greater need and a bigger view.

We naturally feel fear when facing the unknown unknown or even the known unknown because we might not have the programming which would tell us how to handle this new situation. Sometimes we might even feel fear when facing the known known if our previous experience of a similar situation had been difficult, unpleasant or painful. Take, for example, a visit to the dentist or the need to take an exam. Courage allows us to overcome fear, despite the actions of an imagination that no doubt can manufacture images of "the worst possible scenario."

There are two kinds of fear: rational and irrational. It is natural to be afraid of heights when standing at the edge of a precipice but irrational if the only elevation in sight is the curb of a sidewalk. It is natural to be afraid of the unknown because until it becomes known we do not know if we have the tools, knowledge and experience to handle it. We might not know if it presents a threat to our health and existence or not. It is natural to be afraid of the dark because we cannot see what threats it might contain. So a small night light to illuminate one's surroundings at night can be a fitting solution for someone who is afraid of the dark. Once you can see that there is nothing dangerous in sight, fear will retreat.

One transition into the unknown that every person who has ever been born has to face is death and the process of dying. We do not know what awaits us behind the veil that separates us from the "other" world. Being afraid is a natural response to the unknown. Faith and belief can give a person courage and assuage their fear of death. This is why people who subscribe to religions and belief systems that incorporate convictions about what will happen to them after the death of the physical body have less fear about their future fate.

Courage is like an armor that allows a person to defend themselves against the unknown. People who embark on a journey through the wilderness (whether land, sea, desert or jungle) need courage to be able to tackle the unexpected and find ways to survive. Going into unfamiliar territory, whether literally, or figuratively, as in meeting new people, starting a new career or a new job, is to put oneself in the way of courage. The energy of courage awaits the brave people who would venture into the unknown, and will help them transform the unknown into the known.

A young man in native American tribes was called a brave. At puberty he would have to summon his courage (note: we do not manufacture courage; we summon it) and conquer his fears as he would embark on his vision quest. Often alone, in a forest, on a mountain or in a natural environment, he would be exposed to the elements and surrounding wild life. Only then would he truly become a man and a warrior.

The vision quest can still become part of one's life

journey and any person alive has the option of facing their demons and their fears, and becoming courageous. It does not have to be at puberty; one can embark on a vision quest at any point in one's life. In vanquishing fear, a person not only gets rid of their fear; they gain a residue of the quality of courage as well.

The best way to connect to the quality of courage is to act as if it has already happened and that courage is already one of the qualities in one's garden of qualities. This can be achieved through the power of the imagination and the strength of the mind. Courage awaits the person who summons it and attracts it into their energy field. Intellectually we might understand that here is no need to fear what cannot be avoided, but to follow through on that understanding requires courage. We also might understand that there is no need to fear a situation (or person) we need to confront if we want to achieve our dreams and fulfill our destiny. If and when we do, courage becomes a protective armor and a stepping stone into the next stage of our lives.

Exercise

If you are afraid of an exam or a job interview, for example, imagine yourself in the future—beyond the exam or the interview—with a diploma, certificate or job offer in hand. If you are afraid of an operation, imagine yourself in the recovery room with the doctor telling you how well your operation had gone and how you will no doubt return to health in record time. Then, when the time comes for your exam, interview or operation, you will have already created the energy for you to join on the other side of that experience. This should make it easier for you to pass through the challenge you are facing without excess angst or worry.

COURAGE

Courage is to break out of our cage,
To take life by storm, to fully engage,
To do what I have never done before,
To try something new and still look to do more,
To take on a cause, and start a just fight,
To correct an injustice, to make things right.
Courage is an attempt to change and renew,
To open up the birdcage to a wider view,
To see what is right and what is still wrong,
To be one's own person and sing one's own song.

Honor

Honor is a commitment to hold to our word and priorities,
as set out from our core.

CHAPTER TWELVE

Honor

*H*onor is a word that has somewhat fallen into disuse over the past centuries. Medieval knights were all about protecting their honor and championing the honor of their ladies. "Upon my honor" was a common expression, and both gentlemen and ladies were expected to behave in an honorable way.

To this day judges in the United Kingdom are referred to as "Your Honor" and members of parliament are given the title "Right Honorable," whether they are truly honorable or not.

What does it mean to be honorable? Being true to one's word is one aspect of being honorable. If everyone behaved in an honorable way, there would be no need for so many contracts and lawyers, and litigation would be scarce.

Honor is coming back. It has been absent for far too long. People who understand and are sensitive to the unseen worlds know that honor is a frequency that allows other qualities to live and flourish in one's energy field. Honor is a prerequisite to connect to higher energy realms. Angels, nature spirits, fairies, healing essences and elementals see honor as a light that appears in a person's aura and is an invitation for them to communicate and interact with a person. Without honor a person's energy field can easily become polluted, murky and lose the natural luminescence and vibrancy that honor supports. Honor is like a catalyst to good energy. To be right honorable—not in the human-created parliament, but in the energy worlds—is to enter through the energetic gate beyond which magic, healing and revitalizing energies live.

The main aspect of being honorable is being true to oneself, whatever that turns out to mean for any individual person. To become truly honorable is a learning process. It requires a person to listen to their body, instinct, brain and internal spirit guide promptings. It is difficult, for example, to honor one's body if one feeds it foods that are not good for it and cause unhealthy cravings, like sugar or too much alcohol. It is hard to be honorable if one feeds one's brain with thoughts that belong low down the energy realms, like thoughts of lust, hate, vengeance or jealousy.

Keeping one's word and "My word is my bond" are both expressions associated with honor. A person who does not give their promises or their word lightly and endeavors to fulfill their self-chosen and self-imposed obligations is trying to match their intentions with their actions. It is indeed honorable to do so.

When we want to honor someone, whether they are alive or whether we wish to celebrate their memory, we create a ceremony inspired by the person's life, works and character. A person can be honored with a religious ceremony, or perhaps by creating a cultural event, like a concert or a book reading. Foundations are created to honor the memory of deceased individuals of merit, or perhaps a plaque with a name is posted in a church, synagogue or temple, or within the halls of a university or college.

The expression "doing the honors" suggests that there is a ceremonial aspect to honor. One can create ways to honor oneself with self-ceremonies, affirmations and meditations which are ways to confirm to oneself the values and standards that one has implemented into one's life. Every day is a new opportunity to re-confirm one's chosen path. Just like having honorable intentions used to mean that a young man pursuing a young woman intended to marry her and make the liaison permanent, so being honorable to oneself is a commitment to a dedication and behavior of one's choosing.

In some societies honor is a family or tribal affair and it is considered appropriate behavior to kill or wound another person if the clan perceives their honor has been tarnished. Taking another person's life in the name of honor is, of course, not honor at all, but extreme criminal behavior.

"Honor thy mother and thy father" is a known religious guidance. However, it does not mention how we are supposed to do this. One way we can honor someone is by remembering what they have done for us (in the case of our parents—they have given us life and a start in life) and any qualities and virtues they might have embodied throughout their lives. We can do this privately or as a ceremony, when it can be witnessed by family and friends. According to the author, the best way to honor our parents is to live the best possible life we can, so they can be free from worry about us and be settled and content that we are happy. Isn't that what parents want the most? Happiness for their children? Even if our parents are no longer alive, we can still honor them by living well and becoming honorable human beings.

HONOR

At first honor is to keep one's word,
Then it means to say only what one wants to be heard.
It then becomes a family or tribal affair
Until with compassion it makes sure dealings are fair.
Then it does unto others as it would have things done,
Until it recognizes all humans are one.
At the next level it will fight for a country and a land;
In times of peace it knows its place
and will draw a line in the sand.
At the next stage it will feed the poor
and find those who are lost,
Then it will stand up for high standards,
whatever the cost.
Finally it will want to be human
as humans were meant to be
Expressing qualities of compassion,
forgiveness and humanity.

Joy

*Joy is always hovering nearby, but sometimes we
are departed from its attempts to inspire and please.*

CHAPTER THIRTEEN

Joy

*J*oy is like a guiding light—when it is present it indicates times when a person's life is on track—nothing is missing and no desires are unfulfilled. Joy is a settlement and a knowing that all is well.

Joy can be felt in any circumstance; even within the most horrific experiences one can be overcome with joy. Jacques Lusseyran who was blind from childhood wrote in his book, *And There Was Light* that even in a Nazi concentration camp there was never a moment when he did not feel joy. He was always able to help others, despite the harsh circumstances of his incarceration. Knowing German, he would eavesdrop on the broadcast of German news that the guards were listening to and pass on the latest news about the Allies' victories during the last years of the war, thereby bringing hope and encouragement to the other inmates. Jacques believed that helping others is the most powerful way one can connect to the energy of joy.

Joy can come at the most unexpected times—it can seize one without warning or provocation. At those moments it is a reminder that being alive is a precious gift and that one has mighty friends—other people, the planet, the solar system, nature and the universe. Joy lifts a person up into higher energy realms where worry ceases and pain gives way. It is a medicine of the gods that alleviates suffering and causes a person to become noble and rich beyond measure.

Joy has inspired some great works of art, such as the *Ode to Joy* by Beethoven, a choir piece featured in his Ninth Symphony. C. S. Lewis wrote the book, *Surprised by Joy: the Shape of My Early Life* in which he describes his youthful journey from childhood and loss of his mother to boarding school in England, to the trenches of World War One and to Oxford where he made the decision to embrace the Christian faith. Like Lewis, many people associate joy with their belief in a higher power and with their conviction that they are loved and looked after within a purposeful universe.

Joy is indeed often a surprise because it lives in unexpected places. When we pursue it, it often escapes us. But when we are simply happy to be who we are, to be with whoever we are with and to fully be where we are, joy has a habit of materializing in a shower of gratitude and peace. It enhances a person's day—when it is present, everything looks more beautiful. Colors are brighter, people are more courteous and opportunities unfold before one, as if by magic.

The word joy can also be found in such words as enjoyment and joyful. You enjoy something that brings joy into your life and into your energy field. We enjoy what we love to do; we can also enjoy the results of another person's creative work, like a book, a movie or a performance. Joy can be found everywhere—in the beauty of nature or in the works of man. The key to finding joy is developing the eyes to see it, the ears to hear it and the sensitivity to feel it.

Happiness tends to be fleeting, but joy can be a constant companion. It is a state of mind and it accompanies one's belief in the purposefulness of Creation and one's role within it. To enter the kingdom of joy one has a decision to make: does the universe support your life and provide you with everything the human needs to continue living? Or do you live in a hostile universe? Once this fundamental question is answered and you decide you live in a gentle, benevolent and friendly universe, joy will be waiting to join you on your journey through life, wherever it takes you.

Joy comes from the sense of connection to energies bigger and more powerful than us. It comes from universal acceptance, which is always there, but rarely felt or appreciated. Joy connects us to a greater purpose within which we can play a significant part. It confirms our importance and our humanity; it allows a person to learn from the most challenging adversities and to always have hope, no matter what the circumstance.

With joy, all becomes possible. A joyful person becomes powerful and comfortable in their own skin. They believe in themselves and in the fact that they have a unique destiny to fulfill. With joy there is a sense of belonging—we are here for a reason, not for self gratification or personal gain. Our joyful tasking is to find out what this purpose is and to align our thoughts, actions and feelings to that purpose.

Joy brings with it the understanding and the acceptance that the planet is our temporary home and that there are other worlds where joy is a way of life. This planet could be a world of joy if each person followed their dream and their calling and filled themselves and their energy field with joy.

Honesty

*Honesty encourages a person to speak
and live their truth.*

CHAPTER FOURTEEN

Honesty

Most people, when asked what is honesty, will reply, "Telling the truth." It is very important to tell the truth, simply because if you tell the truth you do not have to remember what you have said to whom. If we tell a lie, there is an energy flare in our aura (as well as an increased heartbeat and increased output from our sweat glands, both of which the polygraph measures). This flare will translate into a feeling of uncomfortability until we are able to "own up" to the truth.

There is a saying, "Truth will out." This is mostly true and it is always best to admit to one's actions, mistakes or failures, rather than having them pointed out by someone else. If we hide our mistakes, we might expend unnecessary energy worrying that we will be found out. Sometimes a person might subconsciously help this process of revealing the truth by leaving, for example, a letter in plain view or forgetting to hide the evidence of their deceit. This is because the person is uncomfortable with the lie and the semi-conscious brain causes them to ease the internal pressure caused by the deception by revealing the truth.

How aware are we of the truth of who we are at any given moment? Do we color the truth in our favor when we relate a story from our past? And do we remember events and situations from our own viewpoint, which might be completely different from the truth of someone else who had also witnessed or participated in the same event? How many times have you argued about the truth of a memory or an encounter, only to agree to disagree because the event had occurred in the past and had been relegated to history so it was impossible to check out who was right and who was wrong? Sometimes the best outcome that can be reached when two people remember an event or encounter differently is to agree to disagree.

How can we know if the truth we believe in and are convinced is real, is really the truth? In his book *Blink* Malcolm Gladwell describes an experiment in which a number of people were shown a video clip of an altercation between a group of young men, white and black, on a subway. In the clip one of the white men pulls out a knife. Yet some witnesses said later that the knife was brandished by one of the black men. This demonstrates how our truth is subject to our biases, prejudices and beliefs. We also color our truth with our wishes and desires. If, for example, a person longs for a relationship, they might see the person they are dating through rose-colored glasses, ignoring their flaws, like, for example, their alcohol addiction or tendency to have dramatic mood swings or even their tendency to be cruel. When they discover later that this person is totally unsuitable as a partner and a parent, it might be too late to find someone who is more suitable.

How many times have you heard conversations repeated where the other person's utterances are related in shrill or angry tones, whereas the words of the reporter are repeated in a calm and controlled voice? How true to the facts are these stories?

"Now be honest," we might say to a child or a friend while we encourage them to admit to a misdeed or own up to a wrongdoing. How often do we say the same words to ourselves? The decision to tell the truth to the best of our ability might be one of the most important decisions to make when attempting to grow one's garden of qualities.

A deeper look at honesty reveals that it is much more

than just speaking the truth. Honesty to self has many levels. We have a limited view of ourselves because we cannot see ourselves as others see us or as we truly are. It is inevitable that we have a biased view of ourselves. Another person sees only a fragment of who we are because they are not with us 24 hours a day. Even if they were with us all the time, they still would not know our every thought and every emotion. This is why two different people who know us might have a completely different view of who we are and identify us with different qualities.

We are the only ones who have heard everything we have ever said every day of our lives. How honest were those utterances? Even when we were not lying, we might have been coloring and flavoring the truth as we saw it. There have been many experiments which prove that our memories are deceptive and that we interpret what we see according to our beliefs, prejudices and past experiences.

If we could watch a movie of our every movement and every encounter, we would no doubt have a different view of ourselves than we already have. But even a movie would not show the entire truth. There are always different points of view, different angles of perception. A camera placed in one position will demonstrate a truth that is different from the truth of a camera placed in another. One can never really know the full truth of any situation.

Ours is not the only truth. To be honest we must admit that we can only be honest to our own feelings and thoughts as best we know them. To be honest is to be open to other points of view. Nobody is honest all the time. We all have secrets or false memories, and events from the past that we would prefer to keep hidden from view.

There is a saying—to be brutally honest. It speaks of giving another person a reflection about them, their behavior or about their work. Being brutally honest can be painful for the recipient of this truth, especially if it is not requested; it might be counter-productive and cause more hurt than good. So sometimes it is wise to not be totally honest and to reserve one's opinions to oneself. If someone asks you what you think about their work, be aware of the sensitivities involved in having someone critique one's work. Try to respond with constructive criticism, which includes suggestions and does not just convey your likes and dislikes. Everyone has different tastes and the fact that you might not like something is of little consequence, because there might be millions of people who do. But if you can point out how something can be corrected or improved and this can lead to an enhancement of the person's work, then you will have performed a service to the person asking for your reflections.

It is not easy to be the critic of one's own work. If there is someone whom you trust and whose opinion you value, then it makes sense to ask them to be honest in helping you to view yourself and/or our work.

In his book *On Writing* Stephen King mentions that it is good to have an ideal reader who is the first person to read one's writing and to give reflections while the writing is still new and as yet unconfirmed by others. In his case his ideal reader is his wife. He knows that whatever his wife says about his work will be motivated by value and by her wanting for him to be the best writer that he can be.

Escape into reality, however difficult or harsh, gives a person a place to start. It will lead you away from fantasy, which can be either rosier and prettier than reality or more grim and depressing. Reality and truth are what they are, but we interpret them in our own unique way according to our knowledge, education and according to what we want. We can never know the full truth of any

160

situation or encounter because we cannot venture into another person's mind and thought patterns. Even with people we know well, we never have the full picture of their history, upbringing and secret desires.

A young child might see an elephant for the first time and say, "I saw this huge cow with a very long nose." The child has seen the truth, but did not yet have a label to put upon what he saw. Words, phrases and our history can in fact prevent us from seeing the truth because our education might not stretch to having a reference for what we are seeing. Or we might dismiss what we are witnessing because we believe we have seen it before, and therefore do not look to see what is new or different about the current situation before our eyes and senses.

Our reality enters our brain and cognizance apparatus through our five senses and through our ability to sense the unseen—our intuition, clairvoyance and ESP. We then interpret our reality through the sieve or filter of our history. This is the stage within which we can decide that we want to escape into reality and become more honest.

How can we do this? How can we be more honest? Here are a few suggestions:

🌻 Do not judge another person. You do not know their filters or their reality.

🌻 Give the benefit of the doubt. If you see something strange or different—note it as strange, different or as a curiosity, but do not jump to conclusions about it.

🌻 Ask questions—you might be surprised why people do what they do and learn from other people's knowledge and experience.

🌻 Be tolerant, especially with little things that don't matter. Don't sweat the small stuff, as recommended by Richard Carlson, Ph.D. in his book of the same title.

161

A Garden of Qualities

❦ Enjoy the difference—the world is a big place with other cultures, religions and beliefs. We can learn from other people and other realities.

❦ Stay in what is real—there is nothing as strange and exciting as reality. It is also there that change and development can occur.

❦ Do not judge yourself. Enjoy your reality, whatever it is because it gives you a place to begin.

Exercise
Ask five friends to list five of your best qualities and five of your worst. Give them envelopes, so they can respond to you without you knowing who wrote what.

Charity

Charity enhances the energy field of both the giver and the receiver.

CHAPTER FIFTEEN

Charity

Charity begins at home, the old adage says, and so do all qualities. Can we love someone if we don't love ourselves? Or can we have respect for others if we do not have self-respect?

To give to charity usually means to donate to an organization that helps those less fortunate in the world—the blind, the diseased, the poor, the orphans, the refugees. We need to share our gifts, whatever they are. We do not live alone on this planet and there are always people who need to be taken care of because, for whatever reason, they cannot take care of themselves. There are enough resources on this planet to feed, clothe and house everyone, but something went wrong with the distribution of wealth, so that there are those who have a lot and those who have nothing.

To be charitable is to also give the benefit of the doubt, to assume the best about another person, rather than the worst. To concentrate on another person's best qualities takes effort and a conscious decision, because mostly we have been brought up and educated to be critical. Carping criticism is applauded by our teachers and mentors, and early on in life we encounter the example of satirists, stand-up comedians and professional critics. It is understood that in order to survive in the world we do need to develop our critical faculty. But sometimes being critical is not beneficial to another person; sometimes our honest encouragement and support can better help another person improve and find their true vocation and calling.

A Garden of Qualities

Along with generosity, charity is an antidote to greed. It gives for the sake of giving, like the sun that shines on all equally, whether good or bad. Most religions support the idea of tithing—giving away a tenth of what one earns to support others. This simple action not only helps other people, but it demonstrates an intention to share one's gifts and is an action that makes room for more. To have anything, you must first give it away. Then you can really have it, own it and be known by it. By giving away your talents and your gifts you will improve and have more to give.

The most important kind of charity is to be generous with oneself and to give oneself the room and time to change and grow. This points to a much wider consideration, which is that in order to radiate a quality and to genuinely pass it on to others in one's behavior and feelings, one must apply it to oneself first. This is why in any development process or spiritual journey it starts with oneself first. So what does being charitable to oneself mean or portend? It means, for example, being tolerant when one makes mistakes, as we all do at one time or another. Do you call yourself names when you are found at fault? A mistake is just that—a miss-take or a miss-step, and it does not reflect on one's entire character and life. The fact that I have done something silly or careless or thoughtless does not mean that I am silly, careless or thoughtless. In fact, 99% of the time I might be wise, careful and thoughtful, but just slipped up this once. Also, remember that a mistake is a learning process. Better to try and fail than not to attempt to try. In assessing yourself, take in the whole picture and balance out the unfortunate with the good, as well as the good with the less fortunate.

Another aspect of charity towards oneself is looking after oneself, before looking after anyone else. We can only be charitable to others and offer them our time, energy, as well as finances after we have taken care of our own energetic and health needs. To help others, one needs to be healthy and robust, because it is the overspill of our energetic process that we can most successfully offer to another person. If we expend all our energy on helping others (as many mothers and caregivers do), we will become run down and eventually will become unable to give our energy away at all.

The next level of people that we extend charity to is our family and our loved ones. They should be high on our list of priorities, but as often happens, we are more charitable to distant acquaintances and even strangers than to our own family. Family here can mean not only one's blood family but above all, one's soul tribe. These are people who do not take from us energetically so that we feel depleted every time we meet. They are people who do not give to us in such a way that we might feel exhilarated after meeting them while they feel drained and exhausted themselves. The relationship with our soul tribe is balanced—with give and take on both sides. These are people who inspire you and who are inspired by you. There is a third field that forms up between you and your soul tribe so that both parties become charged and enhanced following a meeting or an encounter. So be generous and charitable to your soul tribe and you will find that they are generous and charitable to you.

Charity then extends to others. Giving is an important part of charity. To grow the quality of charity it is important to give to those who are less fortunate than we are. To make a more conscious decision about how you want to donate to those who need help—research your local charities and decide for yourself who you wish to help and when you are able to do so. So rather than succumbing to outside pressure, like phone calls soliciting donations for worthy causes, make your mind up how and to whom you want to give and which is a worthy cause. Do some research because some charities spend most of the donations they receive on administrative expenses and very little finds its way to support those who are needy and should benefit from your generosity most. Another benefit of going through this process is the fact that once your decision is made you will not use up unnecessary energy being swayed by the persuasive language of volunteers or employees who are reading a script at the other end of the phone and are trying to persuade you to donate to a cause that might not necessarily be high on your list of priorities. So as a result you will be helping a cause you feel is worthy of your support and you will also be saving your valuable energy. By choosing carefully who you wish to donate to you will be charitable both to others and to yourself.

Exercise

Sit down and make a list of people who you feel are your soul tribe. These are people who you might not meet for months or even years, but when you get together again, it is as if no time has passed and you can pick up where you had left off with ease and delight.

Once you have your list, keep these people close to you—in your mind and in your heart. Try to do something a little bit extra for them, whether it means giving them your time, sending them messages from time to time or by making an occasional extra phone call for no apparent reason.

Warmth

*Warmth is a glow of encouragement that enhances
the energy exchange in all our relationships.*

CHAPTER SIXTEEN

Warmth

*H*uman warmth is the kind of energy that occurs between people who have endearment for each other. It makes a person feel wanted and cherished and it warms the heart. It is not physical warmth, though it can help increase the body's temperature. It is an energy within which much richness can happen. It is a catalyst to human exchange. When there is warmth between people, honesty can follow. It allows the baring of the soul so feelings and thoughts can be shared that otherwise might remain hidden for fear of ridicule or censure.

Warmth also allows for that special kind of humor that erupts spontaneously. Words that otherwise do not seem funny at all acquire an effervescent quality—the mind quickens and sharpens and words are understood almost before they are spoken. Warmth lubricates dealings and even in a difficult situation, where there are disagreements or misunderstandings, warmth allows for these to be seen and treated as temporary impediments that can be easily dealt with and resolved between friends.

Sometimes warmth can spontaneously occur, when, for example, one is dealing with a child or someone who needs our support and protection. Sometimes, however, it needs to be manufactured. The way to do this is to remind oneself of one's value for the other person one is going to be dealing with. Warmth works hand in hand with value and respect.

Familiarity is the enemy of warmth (as well as the enemy of respect). As mentioned in the chapter about respect, the root of the word familiarity is the same as in

the word "family" because one tends to be most familiar with those one is closest to. If we live with someone
and see them on a daily basis, we get to know all their
idiosyncrasies and little ways. On the one hand we may
develop endearment for their foibles but on the other
there is always the danger of becoming familiar with our
loved ones and of assuming they will always be there. This
familiarity comes into focus when, for example, we lose
a parent or when a partner leaves. We then think of the
times when we might have been not as warm or charitable
as we would have liked to be.

To avoid regrets, it is a good idea to put in place
practices that can increase warmth, especially if there is
a value and respect for the other person that is perhaps
not always voiced or expressed. Birthdays, Christmases,
Valentine's Days, Mother's Days and Father's Days are
times when value is usually demonstrated and the giving
of flowers, presents and cards allows a person to convey
their feelings on a wave of warmth. However, there are
another 360 days in the year and it is at all times, not
related to any traditional celebrations, that to receive a
demonstration of warmth can brighten another person's
day or week and convey to them a bucket-full of warmth.
It does not have to be anything big or expensive—we all
probably have too much "stuff" anyway. But a little note, a
kind word, even a smile and a touch of a hand can convey
warmth and work its miracles.

Warmth is a healing property. It allows negative
emotions to be dissolved and soon forgotten. It brings an
energy that can become host to natural powers, such as
compassion or empathy.

Some people seem to have a natural warmth about
them that others feel and appreciate. They seem to
be imbued with humanity and are usually sensitive to

the well-being of others. Other people, if they wish for warmth to dwell with them, may need to practice it and by their actions and words invite it into their energy field.

One practical way to become a person of warmth (rather than a warm person—the difference being the deliberate processing and dispensation of the energy of warmth) is to spend time (each day on a regular basis) dwelling upon the strengths and qualities of the people who are close to you. One can be warm to one's family, but one can also be warm to the planet, to the energies that support our life and to everything that surrounds us.

Look around you, wherever you might be—whether in your home, at work or somewhere in nature. Everything supports your life. Your parents gave you life, your environment provides everything you need to continue to live. There are energies and forces that specifically are there to ensure that all life has a chance to continue. It is a great blessing that we are given our days within which to act and think and do. The least we can offer in return is our gratitude and our human warmth which is an energy that enhances our surroundings. We have the unique capability to provide the conductivity for these essences that support human life to do their job and fulfill their destiny.

The planet needs human warmth for her continuance. We are alive at this time so we can fetch for her the warmth of the sun, the planets and the stars. Although she does receive these directly herself, human beings are processing antennae and we are capable of connecting to forces and energies that are higher than planetary level. We have the unique capability to process warmth arriving on planet Earth from the universe. It would be very wasteful not to process these higher energies, but that is exactly what happens when such vices as greed or jealousy hold a person in their grip.

A Garden of Qualities

When we look at the stars on a clear night, we are not only seeing the starry realms; we are also receiving their energy. Perhaps it is not so easy to feel the radiation of the stars as it is to feel the warmth of the sun, but we receive it nevertheless. It might take light years for starry energy to reach the planet, but we are currently receiving energies from the stars that had left their point of origin thousands, millions or even billions of years ago. Having received it, it is up to us to pass it on and to translate it into the noble human qualities, such as love, patience and warmth.

Exercise

To experience the effect of human warmth, pick two similar leaves off a bush or tree. Put one leaf in a drawer or closet and deliberately forget about it, while keeping the other leaf by your bed and sending it warm energy of love, encouragement and value. After three or four days compare the two leaves and see which has lasted better and longer. (You can also try this with two jars of rice.)

Love

Love is the adhesive power that holds the universe together and creates bonds of endearment between people, places and things.

CHAPTER SEVENTEEN

Love

*L*ove is the ultimate devotion. True love is an energetic connection to all that is, whether we are conscious of it or not. It is all-encompassing in its non-discriminating, non-judgmental embrace. It is the fire that nourishes and the cool breeze that relieves pain. It sets things right and shines a light where darkness had previously prevailed. It brings forgiveness and understanding and encourages another person to be themselves. If two people truly love each other, they will each give the other person their freedom to be with them or not, because their main concern is that their partner will choose to do what is best for them. As their feelings for each other grow and as their love sublimates into higher energetic realms, it will become accompanied by such energies as unconditional trust, honesty and loyalty. Such love is rare and where it does appear it should be cherished and cultivated, because this is an energy that can bring balm and healing to the human condition.

Love has many levels and can connect to many levels of energy. Throughout history and in literature the word love has been overused, abused and misused. A person can love ice cream, or a bike ride or a pop group. They can love their dog or their partner or their job. They may love to dance or eat or run. In all these examples the word love is used, and yet each of these expressions of love manifests in different ways. Love can mean many things to many people. Real love is unconditional but even these two words—unconditional love—have been overused and misused to the point where they have lost their meaning.

A Garden of Qualities

Love is an energy that lifts a person up into the higher levels of the energy worlds. It gives of itself and asks for nothing in return. When it gives, it grows, even if the recipient of love does not see it, recognize it or understand it. Love is the great multiplier because it enhances other energies, like patience, peace or courage, and ensures that they too are added to and increased.

The opposite of love is not hate, though it is often said that it is. The opposite of love is the absence of love or indifference. This absence creates a space where negative energies can enter and take up residence within a person's energy field. This vacuum is then an invitation for other low energies, like hate, to occupy the space abandoned by love.

Love is the most natural energy in the world. The universe and the natural worlds are full of love. Only the human specie lacks love and most people long for more love in their life. But when it appears and when it radiates out from a human aura, it is of the purest energetic quality. It is an atmosphere within which great art and great deeds can appear and flourish.

The word *loves* anagrams to *solve*. Love is the solution to most misunderstandings and arguments between people. It is a balm within which disagreements can be settled and solutions to problems can easily be found.

Love not only solves the tangled webs of human dealings, but it also fosters an environment within which geniuses are formed and shaped. It allows people to excel at what they do and to become creative in their work and art. No one needs encouragement or discipline to continue doing what they love. Love is the engine that propels the artist and the writer to keep creating his or her art.

"What do you know about beauty?
It is the shape of love."

Cyprian Kamil Norwid
Polish romantic poet
1821-1883

Man-produced beauty is made by people who love what they do. Their love overspills into their art which they create to share their gifts with the rest of the world. The museums of the world are filled with the evidence and end results of love.

Love can be overpowering and all-encompassing. It can result in physical symptoms—sometimes love causes a person to lose sleep and appetite. It is a quality that to some is worth sacrificing one's life for.

Love is a propulsion to action because we do not like to be separated from the object of our affection, be it another person, an activity or a place. Love is the glue that brings a person close to their destiny and their calling.

When things are difficult or when a person feels lonely and unloved, it is helpful to remember that love is an energy that is always there, waiting for an acknowledgement and an invitation into one's energy field. We are loved and supported by every breath we take and in every waking moment while we are alive on this planetary host we call Earth.

> *To all the questions, love is the answer.*

LOVE

At first love is an arrow, received in the heart,
It gives life new meaning and heralds a new start.
Then it challenges and makes me improve,
It shows me the way to change and move.
It further brings together relationships new
And banishes familiarity,
causing me to refresh and renew.
The world becomes home in a new revealing way,
It makes me more open; it enhances both work and play.
The next level makes me value the fact that I can create,
Thus becoming closer to God and to a godly state.
It opens up vistas never before seen—
In this visionary world I am equal to a queen.
It then brings me back to earth and the land of the living
Where it ushers in generosity and a need to keep giving.
Further it explains it is not here for me alone
But can be found in everything living—
a plant, tree or stone.
Everything is connected and everything the same—
When I pick up a shell it is still part of me
So really I am the one who needs to be tamed
Love helps me understand the truth and to better see.

Love is the glue that binds us together—
Firm like a rock, but light as a feather;
Perfect like a flower and with grace like a dancer,
To all the questions love is the answer.

Part Three

Extras

Introduction

*T*he following poems were written with the idea that there are many levels of perception as far as qualities are concerned. When you think of a quality, the first understanding that comes to mind is one level. But when you start thinking about it more deeply, you come to realize that there is much more to understand about it than you at first might have thought possible. Thus writing about a quality can be a never ending search and discovery that will lead a person from level to level and from understanding to understanding.

These poems are attempts at pursuing such a search and trying to find new levels of perception that will then lead to further discovery and new questions. The results are never definitive, for there are many ways of looking at an object, a situation or a quality. There is no right or wrong in this, but these poems will hopefully promote and provoke the reader into finding his or her further perceptions and understandings.

Take, for example, a vase. It can be seen as a receptacle for flowers, or it can be used to hold water, or it can become a storage place for other objects, like pens or knitting needles. It all depends how you look at it. Of course, interpreting physical objects has its limitations and usually there are only a few uses we can put any object to at any one time. However, as far as qualities are concerned, there are many ways of looking at each one and no two people have the same experience of that quality. Therefore, if asked, each person would probably come up with a different definition of any quality one would care to mention.

These writings are the author's attempts to find further definitions and new ways of looking at such qualities as peace, forgiveness, sublimation or generosity. It is like peeling off layers of an onion, always finding something new to think about and something new to understand.

This exercise is like climbing a ladder of perception and the interesting thing about it is that the higher you go, the greater the similarity between these qualities. It is almost as if there might come a point when all these qualities merge into an unseen plasma that allows a person to connect to higher states and to better understand the manifestation of the divine on Earth. If such a level of understanding were to become accessible, words would no longer be necessary to describe these qualities, because they would become integrated into one's energy field.

In the meantime, searching for new descriptions of known qualities is a noble pursuit, leading to new revelations and new understandings.

FORGIVENESS

At first I regret the many wrongs I have done,
Then I am sorry and wish they would go away—
each and every one.
Next there's an apology
and the attempt to reconcile.
So we make up and end it with a smile.
I then resolve— "this I will never ever repeat!"
I recognize my mistakes
and give myself a clean sheet.
I then have value for all that I have learned,
And see that mistakes made
are lessons honestly earned.
At the next level the quality mercy
dropeth like rain from above,
So I learn to say thank you (merci)
and deal with my weaknesses with love.
Finally atonement lives with me for real
As I learn about forgiveness
and how to start fresh and heal.

LEADERSHIP

At first a leader is a searcher, looking for a way;
Then he makes a decision
what to discard and what will stay.
Next he brings together
the threads that will last;
Then he holds the best of a person
from the future and the past.
Further he creates an ecology
within which others can win;
He then becomes a visionary
and makes many plates spin.
Then he guarantees the level he will not go below;
At the next level he connects to high essences
that by contagion can grow.
Then he allows others
to make their own mistakes,
Like a patient parent,
he knows what development takes.
Finally he responds to the universe
according to needs
And leads by example—he is a planter of seeds.

TRUST

At first trust means I surrender to sleep
and believe that I will awake.
Then with deliberation I choose who to trust and why
and which path is best to take.
Consequently I begin to trust myself—
to be true to my word and deed,
Which leads me to trust that I will be there
in a friend's greatest hour of need.
With increased vision I trust I can help the world
and see what I can best do.
With experience I trust my visions
and that they will one day come true.
Then will I trust the rules
by which my life can well progress;
This encourages me to trust that I should
do more of what I do best.
Then I trust the time has come
to review the status quo,
And finally I trust the gods
to direct me where I next should go.

PEACE

At first peace is the absence of stress
"I need some peace," we may say in distress.
Then again it appears
when you do what you do best—
It is you and it, oblivious to the rest.
Next you can find it in special secret places;
At the next level it lives in loved ones
and those dear, remembered faces.
"Rest in peace," you will say
as you bid them farewell
And gather in shared grief, with stories to tell.
Or "Peace be with you" at the time of goodbye
As you part and depart, with a tear and a sigh.
It then springs to action as it heals,
refreshes and renews;
Next it becomes creative
and inspires like a Muse.
When ready, it emerges into the world
to influence the written and spoken word,
To then incarnate into deep and powerful truths
that are rarely ever heard.
As it grows in power it brings an end to wars
and makes people come to their senses;
It will finally prevail
as we learn to trust it and lower our defenses.

UNDERSTANDING

At first understanding wants to be understood;
Then it examines what it can
and what it should.
Next it looks out to see a large world out there,
So it comes to sense others and learns to compare.
Then it puts itself in the picture
and looks for a plan,
Causing it to look in the mirror and see that it can.
Then it appreciates the unseen worlds
in its domain,
So that it may understand that
no two moments are the same.
Next it takes a higher view
to see what is right;
And finally it dedicates itself
to bring light into the night.

FREEDOM

At first freedom is the ability to do;
Next it takes something that exists
and makes it brand new.
Then it gives rise to alliances present and past,
Which will bring relationships together that will last.
Then it announces itself and stakes a claim,
To become a slavery to its chosen aim.
Gathering strength, it opens up horizons new,
To be able to connect to qualities
accessible to few.
It then acquires the power to protect
and serve the mission of its choice;
Finally it gives to receive
and knows the meaning of rejoice.

HOSPITALITY

At first I invite you to come round;
When you do, I listen to your words
and am sensitive to your sound.
So then I receive your radiation
in a same-same understanding way,
And try to say what I mean and mean what I say.
Next I fulfill your wish
and share with you what is mine,
So I can anticipate your need at a level that is fine.
This teaches me to have value for what lives
behind your eyes,
So that I am open and ready for a good surprise.
Next I try to be colorless,
allowing you to be free to be you;
And finally I see a spirit in everything you do.

SUBLIMATION

At first it means to try to improve,
And so it will challenge, question and move.
Then it connects distant and separate parts;
Next it inspires through healing and the arts.
Then it is an initiative that will see it through;
Intuitively it suggests there is much more to do.
Then it becomes clear life is a journey with an aim,
So it makes an attempt to align with the Universe
and become same-same.
With this there is the responsibility
for every thought and deed;
And finally life is a prayer
in response to Creation's needs.

ART

At first art is everything and everything is art;
Then it educates
and there is a message it attempts to impart.
Next it distills the best
from any art form known,
To then add inspiration
and a quality that is all its own.
At this point it influences the world
to be a better place;
Then it reaches for the future
and creates a new mental space
for understanding and revelation
that then become norm.
At the next level it advances again
to create original content and form.
Finally it becomes timeless,
surviving through countless generations,
And is history in the making,
as it elevates and moves nations.

The journey towards a quality life continues...

www.ingramcontent.com/pod-product-compliance
Lightning Source LLC
LaVergne TN
LVHW011157080426
835508LV00007B/448